SLEEPING IT OFF IN RAPID CITY

Sleepi

AUGUST KLEINZAHLER

g It Off

in Rap

POEMS, NEW AND SELECTED

FARRAR STRAUS GIROUX NEW YORK

l City

FARRAR, STRAUS AND GIROUX
18 West 18th Street, New York 10011

Distributed in Canada by Douglas & McIntyre Ltd.
Printed in the United States of America
First edition, 2008

The new poems in this collection originally appeared
in the following journals: *London Review of Books*,
The Paris Review, *The Threepenny Review*, and *The Times
Literary Supplement*. Several of the poems also appeared in
the following pamphlet: "Traveler's Tales:
Chapter 34," Dia Art Foundation/Discussions in
Contemporary Culture, Beacon, New York, 2005.

Library of Congress Cataloging-in-Publication Data
Kleinzahler, August.
Sleeping it off in Rapid City : poems, new and selected /
August Kleinzahler.— 1st ed.
    p.   cm.
ISBN-13: 978-0-374-26583-0 (hardcover : alk. paper)
ISBN-10: 0-374-26583-6 (hardcover : alk. paper)
I. Title.

PS3561.I38285S57 2008
811'.54—dc22

2007041926

Designed by Quemadura

www.fsgbooks.com

1   3   5   7   9   10   8   6   4   2

The author wishes to thank *London Review of Books*,
the Maker's Mark Distillery, and the Smith-Corona
Typewriter Company for providing (1) oxygen,
(2) courage, and (3) smooth, crisp action.

FOR SARAH

It's the yellow of Cádiz, but a shade brighter;

the rosiness of Seville, but more like carmine; the green

of Granada, but slightly phosphorescent like a fish.

Havana rises up amid cane fields and the noise

of maracas, cornets, bells and marimbas . . .

FEDERICO GARCÍA LORCA

Translated by Christopher Maurer

CONTENTS

I

I

On a 700 foot thick shelf of Cretaceous pink sandstone
Nel mezzo . . .
Sixth floor, turn right at the elevator
"The hotel of the century"
Elegant dining, dancing, solarium
Around the block from the Black Hills School of Beauty
And campaign headquarters of one Jack Billion
("Together we can move forward")
The exact center of the Oglala known universe
Cante wamakoguake
Or only 30 miles or so away, southwest, off Highway 87
I waken to the sound of the DM & E
Rattling through this sleeping town
Sounding its horn as it snakes its way through
Hauling coal from nowhere, through nowhere, and then some
Old rocks and distance, a few hawks overhead
4 a.m.—*per una selva oscura*
—*Kwok, kwok, kwok*, shrieks the velociraptor
In the closed dinosaur shop
                              —*Vroooom*
Roars the Triceratops, like Texas thunder
They keep the tape-loop going through the night

Always have done, no one knows why
The Bible Store respires in its sanctum
As if in an outsize black glass humidor
This is a sacred ground, a holy place
4 a.m. in a sacred place
I can tell this is a sacred place, I needn't be told
It's in the air
I feel it
This old heritage hotel, this is a sacred place
The tour buses are lined up outside it
Awaiting the countless pilgrims
On the floor, my shoe, under the bed
Even my shoe is blessed
The Lord's blessing is everywhere to be found
The Lambs of Christ are among us
You can tell by the billboards
The billboards with fetuses, out there on the highway
Through the buzzing, sodium-lit night
Semis grind it out on the Interstate
Hauling toothpaste, wheels of Muenster, rapeseed oil
Blessed is the abundance, blessed the commerce
Across the Cretaceous hogback
Hundred million year old Lakota sandstone, clays, shale, gypsum
And down through the basins of ancient seabeds
Past the souvenir shops and empty missile silos
The ghosts of 98 foot long Titans and Minutemen

150,000 pounds of thrust

Stainless steel, nickel-alloy-coated warheads

Quartz ceramic warheads, webbed in metal honeycomb

8 megaton payloads

Range 6,300 miles

Noli me tangere

God bless America

We're right on top of it, baby

This is why you're here

Close enough, anyhow, just 11 miles west of Castle Rock

In a pasture, right off 79

The middle of the middle of the heart of this great land

There's a sign

This is a sacred place

Up there in the hills, the vast, ponderosa-feathered batholith

You can see it from space

2 billion year old exposed rock, rising from the prairie

A faint blue shape on the horizon

When approaching from a distance

But seen close at hand "grim and black"

Paha sapa

"Savage cliffs and precipices . . . fantastic forms

Sometimes resembling towns, some castellated fortresses . . ."

A sacred place

Custer once came through, in the summer of '74

With that mustache and golden hair,

And espied here the multitude of flowers
17 varieties in a space of 20 feet
One could pick seven different kinds at dinner
Without ever leaving one's seat
—*It was a strange sight,* he wrote
To glance back at the advancing columns of cavalry
And behold the men with beautiful bouquets in their hands
A sacred place
The Great White Fathers dwell in these hills
Noses and foreheads blasted out of granite
Crazy Horse too, 30 stories high
An enormous pod of migmatite glowering east
Big chiefs everywhere
On every street corner in town
Life-size bronze likenesses
See the chicana brushing President Van Buren, bless her
Bless the chicana in pink rayon, the dutiful city worker
Brushing the statue with a toothbrush in the night
There's Nixon at St. Joseph and 5th
Seated, hands folded on his lap, the way he did
In the midst of "delicate negotiations with Mao"
This is what it says at the base
Bless them, Nixon and Mao both,
Men of peace, soldiers of God
The bronze is cold in the High Plains night

The eyes they gaze out of are holes
Here, at the exact dead center of America
Or close enough, just north of here, off Highway 79
The buffalo roam in these hills
Paha sapa
The bison graze in the shadow of these hills
One angry bull tosses a Harley 30 feet in the air
A big fat biker, attached to it, 30 feet as well
The sacred bison
He would have ridden among the sacred bison, the biker
Ridden as if he were one of their own
—*Tatanka, Tatanka*, cries Kevin Costner
—*Tatanka*, concurs Kicking Bird
—*Tatanka*, agrees Wind in His Hair
Bless Kevin Costner
I saw that one on the wide screen, in Dolby surround sound
Kevin Costner stayed in this hotel
Babe Ruth and Calvin Coolidge too
This is a sacred place
I have come here from far away
After many years of wandering
Disillusion
And found surcease here from all my cares
Surcease here from doubt
Here, at the center of it all

On a great slab of Mesozoic rock
This sanctified ground
Here, yes, here
The dead solid center of the universe
At the heart of the heart of America

SEPTEMBER

The long-beleaguered home team,
black hats and orange piping,
is eliminated on a cool night,
the very end of September,
with the *phlox* zerspalten *by rain,*
as Benn wrote,
and *giving forth a strange animal smell,*
seltsamen Wildgeruchs.

While the neighboring team
from across the Bay,
the ones with green leggings,
younger and more brazen,
were finished earlier still, after the clamor
attending their midsummer surge.

Frucht-und Fieberschwellungen
abfallend . . .
                    Even the strongest
of young arms
tires over a long season.
Tumescences of fruit and fever . . .

Knees give out, just as the parapets
of Troy rear into sight.

What do the sky and gardens know
of such disappointments?
Of the quiet on the street,
life ebbing from barrooms like a yeasty tide?
Go home, everyone go home.
The cupped flame,
the extended sigh of smoke in the shadows
of a hundred doorways.
Go home to your wives, go home.

Why must it always end this way,
every year the same?
It is only we who change, Time
eroding our powers—
des Sommers Narr, Nachplapperer,
summer's fool, jabberer—
putting to rout our boyish hopes.

And even with the air so sharp
once night has settled in—
vor dir der Schnee, Hochschweigen—
when the season's first hearth fires
mingle their exhalations

with night-blooming vegetation,
snow and silence ahead of you,

the sun next day pours down
with such intent as if it could surpass
what only it might emulate,
its counterfeit betrayed
by the very merest wash of bronze

enveloping the Chinese lantern,
jasmine and flowering lavender
in a memorial glow
while, still, they bloom, thrive, reach
up, upwards, toward the light
and out from amidst the withered stalks and ruin
of what summer has left behind.

A HISTORY OF WESTERN MUSIC:

CHAPTER 29

I took a trip on a plane
And I thought about you
I lunched alone in the rain
And I thought about you

One streetcar, then two, disappearing from view
A tortured dream
The fog blowing in, cancelling all that had been
Going street by street
Like a cop on his beat

Over the Great Salt Lake
Yeah, I thought about you
But when I pulled down the shade
Man, I really got blue

I snuck a peak at the clouds
Muttered something aloud
Something I once said to you

We do as we have to
I thought about you

(after Johnny Mercer)

ABOVE GOWER STREET

Rain   a cab   you
Standing there on the sidewalk, in the dark
The gathering thrum as the city awakens

A field of clouds below
Below the clouds the sea
On the screen overhead a movie

Across the great city
They are moving, the two of them
The freeways nearly empty
In pursuit, being pursued
Down ramps, among warehouses
A girl in jeopardy
A beautiful young woman in jeopardy
Before dawn, before the city awakens

On wet streets
The melting greens and reds of traffic lights
A cinematographer's trick with a lens

An access road, the belly
Of a jet, so low overhead

You can read, within its logo
A message:

Why am I here? Who are you?

Because you chose to be here
I am who I appear to be

Across the great city
No, not that one, another
They are moving
Not those two, we
Not you and I
A friend and me, on foot
—*Am I not a friend?*

We are moving slowly
You can track us from on high
An aerial shot
Moving across the plaza
The river to our left, winding
As it does to the Bay
And the giant tower, the sleek green tower
Ahead of us and to the right

Six miles above Godthab
The scent of you

Blooms in the aftertaste
Of the complimentary pretzels
Helio, the deep Atlantic
Titanium white, Iqaliut
Corner Brook a Burnt Umber
The Labrador Sea Cerulean

It is impossible to find a cab
When it rains like this
Come back inside with me
The lighting in the hotel lobby
The black wood panelling and frosted lamps
The darkness outside
I recall this from somewhere
I, other, outside this mise-en-scène
A movie, perhaps

—Who are you?

Night: Burnt Umber mixed with Ultramarine
Cadmium Moon
Clouds a Zinc White
Quebec, on the screen overhead, Green Umber
Ground speed: 1042 kw/hr
Weather at destination: windy

Brick   sky   pastureland
The train moves north from the city
Viridian with Burnt Umber
Prussian Blue with Raw Sienna
Oxide of Chromium Green with Light Red
My friend there waiting, as always
By his car at the station
Ready to drive me back to his valley
With its apron reefs of limestone
Its rucks and folds, its ancient lows
Terra Verte/Phthalocyanine Green
His cat and his piano

   —Am I not your friend, as well?

—Hello. You have 19 messages.
To hear your messages press 1
First message: Where are you?
                Are you all right?
                We haven't had word for weeks
                Are you feeling yourself?

That passenger jet overhead
Where is it going

There on the platform
Making ready for a political rally
The old folk singer
You know this performer
He is doing a sound check
How many times has he done this before
The wind is picking up
Behold, the many banners
The clamor among the faithful
A maple, its leaves an Alizarin Crimson
Deepened and dulled by Indian Red
You are at a latitude you know well
Or did once
You are unaccountably cold

There goes another, overhead
And yet another
Dispatched, it seems, without end
Cutting their engines
Or in steep ascent
Where can they all be going

We are in the north of the country
And in the eastern part
I forget which country
It may come back to me, perhaps not

What time does that make it
You are asleep now, surely

—I want you inside of me

I beg your pardon
Was that you
What was that you said

There are birds out there singing
It is the depth of night
What kind of birds sing at this hour
And in weather like this
Here, come listen
—Those aren't birds, silly
That's only the heat coming up

There goes another plane
Its engines reverberating in the clouds
Now sirens too
Very like the sirens we heard only yesterday
Beside themselves, tearing their hair out
Screaming past us
In that other city
In the rain
In the darkness of early morning

RETARD SPOILAGE

Animalcules heave their tackling,
ladders of polysaccharides,
onto meatmilkshrimp&creamy emulsions,

sticking like putrefactive Velcro.
The refrigerator switches on in the darkness,
a murmuring, perfervid *sadhu* close at hand.

Turbidity, gases, a silky clouding over—
gray slime spreads across hot dog casings,
a sour reechiness transpires below.

However much by day we shore up our defenses,
darling, over time they find their way back
to slowly assail our dwindling larder.

Liquefaction, spoilage and rot—
mephitic flora breed apace,
leaving behind them a ropiness, butyric off-odors.

Ludamilla's prize-winning kraut goes pink.
Fetor of broken proteins—
the drumstick fluoresces, alight with Pseudomonads.

There has to be a music to it all,
I'm certain, if only one could hear it:
a Lilliputian string ensemble's low humming,

an almost inaudible cicada surge,
earwax hissing in peroxide solution,
sausage frying in a distant room.

Good, patient Leeuwenhoek of Delft,
having "partook of hot smoked beef, that was a bit fat,
or ham," of which he was most fond,

suffered a grave ruction below
and so put to work his celebrated lens
that he might better examine his troubled stool

and found there an animalcule, nay many,
but one especially, in the figure of an eel
that "bent its body serpent-wise,"

"a-moving prettily," he made thorough note
in a letter to his estimable coequal, Robert Hooke,
and "as quick as a pike through water."

Sleep, my angel, sleep,
though everywhere out there they are among us,
within, as well, wriggling deep,

they prosper into our dark complement, and by us dwell
in perfect equipoise: your inviolate sweetness
amidst that which is vile&writhing&smells.

A HISTORY OF ~~WESTERN~~ MUSIC:

CHAPTER 49

(MCPHEE'S GAMELAN)

The overtones drift out over the lake
from the direction of the east-facing pavilion,

gathering themselves into a tree of tiny mirrors,
mirrors and gold foil,

suspended above the water's surface—

late sun through heavy foliage,

the clangorous exhalations
dissolving into the low sounds of wind
on water, on nearby *lalang* grass.

Frangipani and incense—
the gods have been summoned:

Sea of Honey, Some False Silver,
Monkey Looks at Himself in the Water . . .

After a slow and chant-like bass
the melody ranges freely, coming and going,

in and out of shimmering arabesques
that ring in the treble as though beaten out
on a thousand wee anvils, xylophones clicking like hail.

—*How shall the gongs be tuned?* asked the smith:
Deep-voiced, in the tuning called "Brave Sea"
or shriller, in the pitch called "Burnt Tamarind"?

—*What is best for the Gamelan of Samara, the Love God?*
asked the other.

—*"A Field of Flowering Pandanus,"*
said the smith, after a moment's thought.
That is the softest and most profound.

Sentences too must float,
if you follow what I mean.

Chopin floats; Schubert, as well.
What is it exactly?
I can't quite put my finger on it.

His eyes met mine in a glance of insolent penetration.
—*The air is salubrious here*, he remarked,
looking out across the valley.

Then there was another tuning,
beautiful and rare.
I had sometimes heard it down by the sea, near Sanur.
The changes among tones very slight,
imparting to the music a sweetly melancholic air.
I believe it is called "the scale of midnight."

Her dishes were endless:
skewers of birds no bigger than bumble bees,
and strangest of all,
small green packages in the shape of cigarettes,
inside them toasted coconut and larvae of dragonflies.

The faint chime of a g'nder
with its floating disembodied sound,
from a nearby verandah:

a single musician playing softly to himself,
waiting for the others to return.

Nutmeg, gardenias, burnt feathers . . .

—*What style!* the old man said,
listening as a tremulous voice rose up, into the air,
above the faint sound of drums.

It was the famous singer from Buleleng—Miss Lemonade.

Kemong, Reyong, Kendang, Trompang, Calung, Gong

Languor and reverie in these chiming tones,
some soft and liquid, some like the notes of a flute,
others full, like the tones of an organ:
perfume, legend, secrecy.

We stood there staring at the water
while a boy tossed scarlet hibiscus into a pool.

Sentences too must float . . .

(Based on fragments from Colin McPhee's memoir, A House in Bali*)*

PORTRAIT OF MY MOTHER IN JANUARY

Mother dozes in her chair,
awakes awhile and reads her book
then dozes off again.
Wind makes a rush at the house
and, like a tide, recedes. The trees are sere.

Afternoons are the most difficult.
They seem to have no end,
no end and no one there.
Outside the trees do their witchy dance.
Mother grows smaller in her chair.

At the Hotel Oblivion, Airport Drive
  Mezzanine, Conference Center B
    PowerPoint presentation #1
Career Enhancement Strategy
Mary-Ray's pink ice service trembles
  In the aftershock of some astral seizure
    So remote and faint
      Only the weevil's foreleg dares say
        Yes, yes, yes, it's true
        Next up
Team Building Exercises
 Woof, woof
   Burgundy carpet, big yellow dots
     That new smell, glycol ethers
       4-phenylcyclohexane in the latex backing
Break: Free Coffee, Light Snacks, Get Acquainted
  Uh, pardon me, Miss Carnoustie
    Is that your panty line
      Or a silken esker of longing
        Have an hallucination, have a bagel
          We had an issue under discussion here
          Regarding the lighting, I believe

That tenebrous strip beyond the chandelier's orb

Hey, help me out here

Not now, Peg, I'm teething

Are we ready for the evening

Thought Shower

Hold on, the jacaranda's gone missing

Waiter, some more Vitamin Water, and hurry

Wow, here comes

36,000 blasts of ink per second

In four, count 'em, four brilliant colors

And with no telltale digital trace

I see a hand up

Mr. Gomez, are we still on the same page?

A southerly buster off of Bass Strait
was raising whitecaps in the Bay
and jittering the flags out across the plaza.
We were sitting under the famous bare-ass portrait of Chloe.
You know the one, in the old upstairs hotel bar, posh.
So _____ says to me, he says . . .
Wait a moment, you knew _____?
Not well, acquainted-like, a snort, or two, or three,
on the way home from the Culture Fair that day.
He's _____, telling me that story of Ava Gardner,
how when she was out here in '58
for the filming of *On the Beach*, they ask her
What do you make of the place, Miss Gardner?
flash bulbs going off left and right,
and she says Perfect,
if you're making a movie about the end of the fucking world.
Whuh . . . whuh . . . what was he like?
Who? _____. Oh . . .
Sardonic, bright, afidget in his hide,
slagging off all and sundry,
not much good to say of aught, they're all like that:
an unwholesome pallor, vigorously earned, I'm sure.

And when was this? I dunno, I dunno:
like everything else, twenty years ago.
A stunned, reverential pause—
they tremble at the altar of that poor bastard,
not least his longtime *friends*, for show;
don't want to be caught out not at Sunday prayer, no, no.
Crikey, seize up at 40 after a long, hard night
and leave a smart, mixed, testy oeuvre behind
they turn you into a smack-addled Apollo,
the home-grown Rimbaud of an entire generation.
Why would none of this have surprised him?
I can see him, sneering into his terpin hydrate,
another fallen, self-lacerating ex–altar boy,
third pew, center aisle, at the Church of Eternal Damnation.

FRIDGE MAGNET NIPPON

[PREFACE]

Ink

Stick

Night

Rub

Drip

Saucer

Light

Thought

Insect

Sleeve

White

Phrase

Wing

Fan

Breath

Hand

[TINY FANS]

Fragile   *comme un lisserand*

Weaver wand   thread of rain

White peony

Less a color than breathing

The scent

Close your eyes

One closes one's eyes

Flash of lightning

Incense

Glycine   *ses mille bras*

Serpent of wisteria

White lantern

Somber thunder

Tomb

The hare lights a cartridge

Again lightning

An abandoned white lantern

Fog

Fog   mixed with crumbs of silver

Dragonflies, countless

Irises among ditchweeds

Irises, like a swarm of young peasant girls

In the center of the peony
 a black bee
      enters and leaves
        voluptuousness
                the supreme javelin of its bodice

Four o'clock in the morning
        blue smoke mixes with memory

How to speak of autumn
        when still the tart sound of the flute
            in spring
                fills my mouth with water

Little by little   rain becomes snow

Ink of joy

Black juice

Mr Cat

Biting down on a hairpin

Glances sideways

[Scrambled and plucked from Paul Claudel's
Cent phrases pour éventails*]*

NOIR

The light emission diodes stare,
incandescent crab eyes.
Foghorns trade calls in the night
as if lost, seeking one another out,
sometimes in the key of A,
sounding out there by the cliffs,
sometimes in G or C,
depending on how the fog is blowing,
but always at their loudest right before dawn.

A fine rain falls.
The actors scuttle back to their trailers
after the hours of hitting their spots,
muffed scenes, take after take,
shivering out there under the helium lamps.
Another crap, overbudget hommage
to Hammett and John Alton,
Magyar master of the shadow game:
fog, steam and smoke,
bad news behind the slatted blinds,
the half-illumined face
and pistol's report.

Exhausted, feeling a little debauched

after too much weasel, cop and tough, good-time Mabel,

down on her luck,

the canny Chinaman named Wu,

three of them play cards,

the other two, after a few lines of blow, screw.

The front is blowing in from the south.

You can taste it in the air,

smell it.

The flags on the downtown buildings begin to snap.

It starts out there on the Pacific,

a thousand miles off the China coast,

and comes across on the westerlies.

That's what it does this time of year.

I've been out here a long time.

Every year.

You can set your clock by it.

The native whites are flat of head,
especially small children,
who bark sharply and spit
at any provocation.
The dark race wears an earthen cast,
a mix of sand and ash,
and look out from under their brims
wary and dazed,
as if for a long time hunted.

Sun Microsystems is at one end,
the bank towers at the other.
In between, terror alerts
are rotated with sportswear ads
on the sides of bus shelters.
If you see or hear anything
out of the ordinary
it is your duty as a citizen to phone . . .
One feels almost at home,
and here so very far away,
another hemisphere,
facing on a distant ocean.

A seabreeze called "The Doctor"
arrives at 6,
along with the stewardesses
in their red caps and gauzy veils,
filling up the hotel lobby
and chattering away like exotic birds.
The purply neon of the bank towers
does something,
something marvelous over the river
with the magenta
of the altocumulus clouds,
vibrating off one another
until the Supreme Court gardens are suffused
in a light, first-spectrum violet,
then Moorish blue, then back again.

—*Dubai sky*,
offers the famous travel writer.
He is standing at my shoulder,
a dark, slight, genial man.
We meet in such places as this.
Every few years we cross paths
far away from home.
Although he seems not really to have a home
except that of airports
and a perpetual predawn realm

lived out alone
in this Asian city or that,
unable to sleep,
walking the streets,
always in search of the red lantern
betokening the entrance to an unforeseen world.

SECONDARY SEXUAL CHARACTERISTICS

[1]

Spindrift of grunion spume in moonlight
Granular, sorrel-colored, ammoniac
Upon the tide's retreat
A meniscus of foam hissing in sand
The milt bores deep

[ii]

His presence was more than unwelcome
The changeroom strictly off-limits
Except for the dancers

Relish of wild duck cooked with olives

The slight scent of prussic acid

A faint whiff of overripe peaches

These impromptu *Etudes endocrines* of his
I can see him now in his velvet waistcoat
Holding court, a bunch of Parma roses
In lieu of a cravat, crowding his throat
And, of course, those miniature barrels of scent
Arranged there on the parlor shelf
What he called his "delicious little pipe organ"
That *treasure* of his revolting sensorium

[111]

Miss Emily Jones Nespith of Roanoke
Lets fall her precious lace hanky
But the gallant lieutenant takes little notice
His attentions elsewhere
Chiefly, in the direction of one Laura Grey Dwight
Who, all agreed, had "blossomed" overnight
But the musk notes of the former's errant gift
Were not lost on the house cat, Pip
Curled behind the skirts of the beige settee

The quadrilles played on
But Pip, Pip was grooving to a limbic tomtom
Head like a bobble-doll's

Eyes like slits
Poor Pip
Drool at his lips
Caught up in a proper fit
A 9-cycloheptadecenone-addled marionette
Mewing
  —Kill me, fuck me, write me bad checks

VANCOUVER

Black filthy rain it's raining
like a grudge is out
but the neon mermaid over the fish place
looks best that way, in the rain.

Downstairs, Sol, of Sol's Paradise Club,
mixes a fizz drink for a mummy blonde.
—*Thanks, Sol.*
The resident "monster on alto,"
recently back from a large success in Regina,
roars through the bebop warhorse "Steeplechase,"
played in the manner of Jackie McLean,
say, around 1957.
                 Everything sounded good in '57.

At the foot of the block is the inlet
and beyond the inlet the mountain
and beyond the mountain almost nothing,
nothing until the North Pole:
                 Squamish,
Far Mountain, Ootsa Lake,
lichen-colored eternities

sprinkled with bear scat,

the abandoned dam project,

an unspeakable *comfort station* along the gravel highway,

Tuktoyaktuk.

It is March.

Tomorrow morning, drivers,

commuting to work along the North Shore,

will observe a dusting of snow

on the branches of cherry trees lining the road,

the same trees now in bud

and making ready to blossom.

Were it not for the Safeway and car dealerships

one or two might think of *Ukiyo-e*

and the great Hiroshige, or perhaps Hokusai.

But tonight, tonight in the harbor below,

freighters queue

                1 2   3   4   5

waiting to dock.

A sailor aboard the lead ship, a Dane,

sniffs the saltchuck and lights himself a smoke.

He gazes out to the shimmering downtown spit.

He likes how tobacco and sea air mix in his nose.

GODDESS

Well now, it really is you,
and after how many months?
I had ceased keeping track.
No, not given up, never that.
I should die if that were true.
But still—was it some affront?
You've never been this cruel.

Distracted? To be sure;
even you can't begrudge me this:
a father, friend, another friend.
Death's visits threatened never to end.
I know better than to implore,
complain, or like some schoolchild, wish.
Unvisited I do not live, I endure.

A VALENTINE: REGARDING THE

IMPRACTICABILITY OF OUR LOVE

Evel Knievel, Robert Craig Knievel of Butte,
now that one, that wild . . .
The crack-up at Caesars Palace in '68,
then trying to clear the thirteen Pepsi trucks in Yakima,
and just down the road, here at the Cow Palace:
You could tell by the way he wore his hair
and the white kid leather jumpsuit with fringe.
An ordinary man doesn't jump the Snake River Canyon
with nothing underneath his ass
but a two-wheeled, fin-stabilized X-1 Skycycle
and a seven-figure guarantee from some *macher* in L.A.

Darling, I've walked away from a wreck or two myself,
or crawled, and earned the name of fool, full sore.
But let's take off this one last time: no net,
no harness, no nothing underneath to break our fall.
Th' animal Spirits that from pure blood arise
are what get us aloft and the fuel by which we fly.
So hold on, baby, we're lifting off.

Don't look down, your head will swim, and don't let go.
Once in the air we're on our own.
They'll all be watching, assembled below.
C'mon, luv, let's give the punters a show.

Shoot the freak Cold wind, boardwalk nearly empty *You know you wanna*
A cluster of hip-hop Lubavitch punks, shirttails out, talking tough *You*
    shoot him
he don't shoot back Keeper-flatties thrashing in buckets, out there on the
    pier
Shoot the freakin' freak A regular family of man out there, fishing for
    fluke
and blues in that wind   *How you gonna build memories*   Everything
    shut down
or gone   *Let the lady have a try* SpongeBob, Spookerama, Luna Park
Shoot 'im in the head   the Mighty Atom, Thunderbolt, Wonder Wheel
He likes it when you shoot 'im in the face   Surf House, Astroland,
    Shutzkin's
knishes, *A real live human target*   "Hungry for Fun," fried clams
Everybody's gonna   "Bump yo' ass, bump bump bump yo' ass"
You know you wanna   You know you wanna   You know you wanna
And that's when we saw him, *him*, 120 million records sold worldwide
walking across the sand   "It's him, it's him" Like a god, with that hair
What does he do to keep it like that   Looking good still, tall, slim,
    creased slacks
handmade Italian boots, a black goddess on his arm, like an older
    version of that chick

on Miles' *Sorcerer* album, wow   The camera crew running all around
   them, frantic
He's waving his arm toward the ocean, telling her how it used to be
how it used to be when he was growing up close by in Brighton
   Beach
OhmyGodOhmyGod "Sweet Caroline," "Holly Holy," "You Don't
   Bring Me Flowers"
the duet with you know who, the two of them in the choir together
   at Lincoln High
the 1992 Christmas special, the White House concert, the time
   he met Lady Di
("a great person, just a fabulous person, a real human being")
I mean how good is this, really, I mean really, seriously, how good
   is this

ALMOST NOTHING

(IN MEMORIAM: GORDON ASHWORTH, ARCHITECT)

They say the great man drank
Ceaselessly
            the way an Englishman drinks tea
An Englishman of a certain class and time
A particular place
On a winter Sunday
A rainswept afternoon
Cup on the hob
Big pink Art Deco ashtray
A little V of plaster ducks on the wall in bas-relief
And the Chinese lady in her yellow *qi pao*

He wasn't English, of course
The great man
But that need not concern us, not here
Rather, how that famous open plan of his
Would abhor these little, closed-off rooms
The dreadful ornament
And narrow hall and three-piece suite
Upholstered in red and green

The mangle one step down
Just off the kitchen

He was said to favor a martini
How otherwise
Sculptural, and sans olive
An object of perfect clarity
Efficient, no waste
The "silver bullet," as some liked to call it
Stream form
Like a bicyclist leaning into a curve
At the Hippodrome
Or along the Rochdale Canal
And up into the Pennines
Open countryside
Tires hissing on wet pavement
Leaving the closed world behind
He would drink them down without end
And no effect
Except in somehow scouring himself
Of waste, of clutter
Clutter of memory, history, adulterated space
Dematerialized
Beinahe nichts, his motto
Almost nothing

For the Chicago heiress
The ungainly spinster who played violin
He glumly romanced
And who so adored him
Her "clairvoyant primitive"
He built a house that seemed to float
Out in the woodlands, by a river
Chaste in its geometry
And made almost entirely of glass
Distilled
And further distilled
Again and again
Like his expensive vodka
Until "light enough to float on air or water"

She hated it, of course
But that was later
Nowhere to sit
Barren, sterile
Bugs all summer
Cold all winter
Roof leaked
That terrible row at the end
Humiliated
Out tens of thousands
Ridiculed by his admirers

His countless admirers
"A modernist Shinto shrine"
Yes, well

—*Stand up there on the terrace*
He said to her
Commanded, rather
—*So that I can have a look at you*
She melted
The house still unfinished
When she still adored him
Her genius
Her darling Plato with his stogie
Gazing down at him
—*Good*, he barked
His accent still strong after 13 years
More like *gut*

And in the other place
The closed-off place
Gracie Fields sang "The Isle of Capri"
Coke and that morning's fry still in the air
Almost impossible to breathe

He didn't say much
That discomfited her

He never said much

That and the drinking

She let it pass

A great man

—*Well*, she said

With a flirtatious half-curtsy

He stared and stared

—*Well*, she said

He was silent a long time

—*Gut*, he said finally

Gut

The scale is gut

The bicycle paths of this *Social Democracy*
are busy with pedallers, humorless and good,
speeding down their privileged corridors,
kinetic emblems of an enlightened state,
efficient, compassionate and *on the go.*

Our visitor shuffles to the *fine arts* museum
and sits there, mildly hungover, before the Delvaux,
not one of his best, as if that really mattered,
finding refuge in the moonlit porcelain breasts
of the recumbent, homely maja, *de* maja *van het noorden*

and the old locomotive that waits, steaming fitfully
in the middle distance.
                              —*T-t-toro, t-toro, t-t-t-toro,*
crackling from the invisible loudspeakers,
or so one might imagine, in a stammering falsetto;
the background sky the kind of purple you find

summer midnights in far northern climes.
Meanwhile, Inspector X engages Inspector Y
in a whispered exchange, a matter of *singular* import,
an unspeakable incident, a clue gone missing . . .
—*What is the function of art in society today?*

barks the guest moderator at today's symposium,
crosstown, the Institute of Higher Learning:
a small, nervous, choleric creature, indeterminate gender,
dressed in what look to be black angora Mao pajamas.
The conversation afterward involves a sharp exchange.

It is raining. It is always raining on days like this,
the gallery nearly deserted but for the museum guard
and our visitor, sitting there on the bench,
as he has been, for what seems like nearly an hour,
maybe more, staring at the painting in front of him.

Outside, in the courtyard, rain falls intermittently
on the grotesquely phallic sculpture in bronze,
a prize acquisition that still raises eyebrows.
Who is to say what is going through the mind
of our visitor, sitting there, stolid, transfixed?

It is often remarked upon, in survey books, compendia,
the *strange and unearthly calm* of these paintings
by the *minor surrealist*, an *enigmatic* Belgian,
even here, and doubtless on the audio guide;
that and what they call his *atmosphere of mystery.*

I WENT TO SEE McCARTHY

I went to see McCarthy

with cardinals rattling in the boxwood
and pecans suffering
their convoluted slumber in the heat,
taproots humming deep underground;

from a parched bare plain of yellow ochre
to a green place, hilly and moist.

And a great sleep overtook me
upon crossing Nacogdoches.

Until next I knew we were dropping,
dropping down through the clouds,
into the rain and old quarrels,

low in sight of Ballymadog
and the cliffs of Knockadoon Point,
the sea, the gray mothering sea,
boiling away among the rocks

and the shrikes circling below us,
and the barnacle geese, piloting us in.

He buttered some bread, McCarthy did
by way of an hello
and bade me sit down by his tall windows
to take in the view of the river below,
the river and tall steeples.
For McCarthy commanded a lofty view,
a view atop a very fine hill,
and the clouds raced in from the west.

—*Have a pat, Jimmy*, McCarthy said.
(Jimmy, he made up his mind to call me.)
Skibbereen's finest, he said.

And the river widened away below,
outside of the tall windows,
it widened to the east and south,
and further still past the old castle,
carrying with it the fishing smacks and freighters,
out to the harbor and open sea,
the harbor and gray, mothering sea.

I went from a dry place, echoless and vast,
a parched bare plain of yellow ochre,
remorseless land, remorseless sky,

remorseless, vast and cirrus-streaked
to McCarthy's kingdom by the sea,
swaddled in cloud, all gray and green,
pasture, bog, hillock and town
swaddled in cloud, all gray and green.

McCarthy was all for tall windows and butter.

—*A pat with tall windows is your only man,*
McCarthy said, and said it not free of pride,
not free of pride in the manner he said it.

Soon enough the dark rolled in,
the dark rolled in and still more rain,
and the city clock read 7,
of several minds the fish-shaped weathervane,
of several minds on a blowing night.

And the rain was full of tales, full of tales,
having drawn them up like water,
like water from the green earth below,
then raining them back down, down and down,
a softly spoken incantation without end.

Outside and in the streets below
the ghosts of Mike O'Donovan and Sean

still covered the leafy Mardyke mile,
young Mick flapping his arms and noisy,
a tall crazed crested grebe in silhouette,
all crackpot opinings and complaint

about the lost art of churning butter
and how it might be regained.
Sean, the quiet one, meanwhile nodding,
the kingdom's future chroniclers,
noisy Mick and the older Sean,
of how it was and when and where,
covering that mile of gravel path,
streetlamps lost in the leaves overhead,
putting it in the air and testing it,
getting what wanted saying said.

—*Have yourself another pat. Go on,*
take another pat for yourself, Jim,
fresh as if served wrapped in cool grass cuttings.
St. Brigit's golden harvest,
fresh as if served on a firm cabbage leaf.

And outside the tall windows
the kingdom's stories did unfold,
like a long and crowded scroll,
a long and crowded scroll,

the many tales of an old small place,
a place long lived in, much traveled through,
a kingdom within a kingdom
on an island in the sea.

Outside there, in the rain,
all history, it seemed, unfolded before us,
through the rain-streaked windows,
in the blackness and the rain.
The 18th century made its stately passage,
it was a procession down Mallow Lane,
down Mallow Lane to the river's quays,
the barques and packet ships filled with good butter,
butter knuckled into seasoned oak firkins,
firkins expertly coopered and headed,
seasoned oak firkins coopered and headed,
and sent off to Zanzibar, Kingston, Cádiz.

And then there was the "Big Fella,"
another chapter to be told, another still,
a much beloved tale it was,
the kingdom's hammer, hammer and champion,
and a lovely broth of a boy he was,
pounding that freckled ham of a fist,
that great resounding freckled ham,
down on the plank, the plank before him:

—*Come along, lads, with me*, he roared.
Come along, lads, with me.
This butter belongs to no one but ourselves
and it's that knowledge and the pike,
the pike and butter shall set us free.

—*Are you having fun?* McCarthy asked.
Are you having a good time? he asked.

—*McCarthy*, I said, *so many tales:*
How is there so much to tell of so small a place,
a place so small as this?
Where does it all come from, and does it never end?

—*Have a pat, Jimmy*, McCarthy said.
It's only the same as your VCR,
the same as your VCR at home.
It all just rewinds and starts over again,
it rewinds and starts over again.
But never the same way twice. And he winked.
Never exactly the same.

—*Fine butter, is it not, Mike?*
(And now he decided to call me Mike.)

—If butter can't cure what ails you,
no cure is there to be found, ha ha,
no cure is there to be found.

And outside, outside the tall windows
the rain continued to fall,
and so too the kingdom's many stories,
one after another they did unfold,
the many stories of an old small place,
long lived in, much traveled through,
a kingdom within a kingdom
on an island in the sea.

The Great Betrayal, the Earls' Retreat,
the Battle of Creamery Knoll:
Many fell there, many a brave one,
and with them a terrible spoilage of butter.

The fever that beset the milk cows,
the dreadful fever that turned the milk.
The drought that withered the silage.
The invasion that cost the land its churns.
So much sorrow, for so small a kingdom.
Many poems were written, many songs sung,
poems written, unhappy songs sung,
and tales too, written by Mick and Sean.

—For as the churning of milk brings forth butter,
McCarthy said dolefully, in a doleful voice,
and the twisting of a nose brings forth blood,
so the forcing of wrath brings forth strife,
brings forth strife, McCarthy said.

I left from a parched bare plain,
a plain burnt zinc-orange, burnt yellow ochre.
I left under a cirrus-streaked sky,
a relentless and cirrus-streaked sky,
where the tales that arise from the land
are blown away like spindrift,
spindrift of yellow sand when the wind arrives.
And those scarce few tales that remain
are grudgingly told, as few words as it takes,
as few words as the telling takes,
rendered sparsely as the rain.

—We have an anthem, McCarthy said,
a song from long ago and in the old tongue.

McCarthy saw fit to translate it,
bless him, my host, he translated it for me
and this is how I heard it sung:

Ohhhhh, a vision once appeared to me
an apparition to amaze.
We came on a ship made all of lard,
and we steered that boat to the open sea,
we steered it to the open sea.

Until we came upon a fort,
its battlements of custard made,
and beyond a lake, a lake we found,
fresh butter was the bridge in front,
and bacon the palisade.

Hedges of butter fenced it round,
Its pillars were of cheese,
behind it was a well of wine,
and whiskey filled its streams.

A very fine place to sup on, it was,
a very fine place to sup,
and a better place still to dream, begob,
the best of all places to dream.

—*Having fun, Bill?*
McCarthy said (and now he called me Bill),

his voice, as it did, going up and down,
in speech, as it did in song,
in speech, as in song,
just like his little kingdom's hills,
just like his kingdom's hills.
And it was a kind of singing, it was,
the way he spoke, his way of telling tales,
that the tales seemed almost like songs,
and every song told a tale.

It was a singing place, McCarthy lived.
Oh, not in the usual way,
not at all like "Eensy Weensy Spider"
and surely not "Up, Up and Away."
Speech was sung and the songs,
the songs were full of talk,
both suited to the telling of tales,
suited to telling tales.
And many tales there were to tell,
for one small kingdom a great hoard of tales,
tales of intrigue and glory and butter,
intrigue and travail.

The tales themselves so sweetly told,
so pleasingly told and well,
because how the tune of them fell on the air,

because of how it fell,
it made no matter if the tales were true,
or whether the reckonings fair,
no matter be they true or fair.
The butter was sweet, that's all I knew,
the tunes and butter sweet.

I went to see McCarthy.

I left from a hot, dry place,
a parched wide plain the color of burnt orange,
where the songs all begin "Giddy-yup"
and end "The skies are not cloudy all day."

I went to see McCarthy
in his kingdom by the sea,
all swaddled in gray and green,
an old, old place with many a tale,
some tales told, others better sung,
a kingdom within a kingdom
on an island in the sea.

Now back from whence I came
it seems all like a dream,
an excellent dream, to be sure,
but far more dream than real.

And much of it now steals from my mind,
much of it steals away.
But two things I'll not forget;
two things planted in my mind will stay:

One is that if something's worth saying,
and sounds good once it's said,
you may just as well just say it twice,
it costs no more or less;
good once, better twice, go ahead.

And the other was something McCarthy said,
he said it by way of a goodbye.

—*Hurry back, boy*, McCarthy said.
Hurry back soon for a pat and good craic.

But the very last thing McCarthy said,
the final words he said:

—*Now, Jimmy, this you must remember,
remember and never forget:*

*Don't stand out in the sun, ever, ever,
(listen up, boy, now you listen)
when you've got butter on top of your head,
butter on top of your head.*

ANNIVERSARY

You'd figure the hawk for an isolate thing,
commanding the empyrean,
taking his ease in the thermals and wind
until that retinal flick, the plunge and shriek—
cruelly perfect at what he is.
With crepe myrtle igniting the streets
and flowering pansy underfoot
I'd get out there just after dawn each day,
before the sun made it over the mesquite and honey locust.
Cliff swallows rocketed low over grass,
dragonflies darted above:
every day, on the heels of first birdsong, juice-heads
sleeping rough by the culvert.
Before the heat,
before the ebb and flow of cicada whir swallowed the world,
when the crepe myrtle was still in bloom,
when it was the flowering pansies' time in the park and untended lots,
and still a touch of cool in the air.
I remember once, a redtail perched close by
on a branch or utility pole.
Maybe he came down for a better look,
but I think it was so that I might better see him,
who reigned over these few acres and beyond

and what it was about him so overmastering.
An ugly sheen encouraged some gold in his russet mantle.
His belly was white.
Look at me, he seemed to be insisting.
Behold, a pure wild heartless thing,
beautiful and horrible, nothing in between.
I one day saw him tearing at his prey:
he was in the crook of a tree, low and close at hand,
fixed on it, drunk with it, mercilessly at it,
the sound like a cleaver tearing through meat,
cruelly what he was, nothing else.
But on another day, not long after, I heard him,
perched high on a branch, calling out,
crying out in distress, piteously,
kee-eeee-arrr, kee-eeee-arrr,
a harsh, descending sound, and unrelenting,
kee-eeee-arrr kee-eeee-arrr,
panicked or wounded, terrible in his dismay,
until, suddenly, from some other corner of sky
another hawk flew down to join him,
not right there on the same branch but on another, close by.
And soon after that, off they flew together,
drifting, spiraling, higher and higher
in partnered loops, wheeling and diving,
enraptured by all they were, were able to do,
not as separate beings, but as two.

II

ON JOHNNY'S TIME

When Johnny goes out
he's careful what gets into his Time.
He likes Time plain,
the better to taste it run out of him
like water out holes
in the Old Town's corroded pipe.

—*What sort of business you in?*
the good burgher always asks John.
—*Monkeybusiness*, is what John likes to tell him,
and won't crack a smile, ever.
That's John.
But when Johnny goes out

on Johnny's own Time
he's out there doing the only one thing:
he's burning off all the stillborn Johnnys
that hatched in his head in the night.
And that John, he won't ever come home,
not until he's right.

No telling where: down the hill
and out of sight—
soapbox derby heroes in a new dimension.
Don't bother to resurrect them
unless some old newsreel clip
catches them shocked
with a butter knife in the toaster.
Countless snaps and episodes in space
once you hit the viewfinder that fits.
It's a lie anyway, all Hollywood—
the Mind is a too much thing
cleansing itself like a great salt sea.
Rather, imagine them in the eaves

among pigeons
or clustered round the D train's fan
as we cross the bridge to Brooklyn.
And make that a Friday night
July say. We are walking past
the liquor store to visit our love.
Two black boys are eating Corn Doodles
in the most flamboyant manner possible.

She waits, trying

to have the best song on as we arrive.

The moon is blurred.

Our helicopters are shooting at field-workers.

The Mets are down 3–1 in the 6th.

MEAT

How much meat moves
Into the city each night
The decks of its bridges tremble
In the liquefaction of sodium light
And the moon a chemical orange

Semitrailers strain their axles
Shivering as they take the long curve
Over warehouses and lofts
The wilderness of streets below
The mesh of it
With Joe on the front stoop smoking
And Louise on the phone with her mother

Out of the haze of industrial meadows
They arrive, numberless
Hauling tons of dead lamb
Bone and flesh and offal
Miles to the ports and channels
Of the city's shimmering membrane
A giant breathing cell
Exhaling its waste
From the stacks by the river
And feeding through the night

Loneliness—huge, suddenly menacing
and no one is left here who knows me anymore:
the Little League coach,
his TV repair truck and stinking cigars
and Saul the Butcherman
and the broken arm that fell out of the apple tree,
dead,
dead or gone south to die warm.

The little boy with mittens and dog
posing on the stoop—
he isn't me;
and the young couple in polo shirts, ready to pop
with their firstborn
four pages on in shortshorts and beatnik top
showing her figure off at 16 . . .
1955 is in an attic bookcase
spine cracked and pages falling out.

Willow and plum tree
green pods from maple whirling down to the sidewalk . . .
Only the guy at the hot dog stand since when
maybe remembers me,
or at least looks twice.

But the smushfaced bus from New York, dropping
them off at night along
these avenues of brick, somber as the dead child
and crimes of old mayors
lets off no one I know, or want to.

Warm grass and dragonflies—
O, my heart.

In the jelly, jam, and haircare aisle of the Waikiki Foodtown
as if in a capsule whose walls bear decals, a shattered fresco
(*Fatty Arbuckle sipping a Coke at the St. Francis Hotel*, etc.)
the Man from Moruya, a world then a world away again from the
    chrysanthemums
at the farm's eastern gate, is turned inward by the Percy Faith Strings'
arrangement of an especial old favorite, "Just Like Tom Thumb's
    Blues"—
iridescent oil pouring from the overhead speakers, lubricating
the sentiment *we're all, each of us, one, softening*
and put somehow more at ease by the very available and
    high-gloss kitsch
the Big Enchilada loves you to hate

or out on the highway, four miles from town, on a stool in the
    Snack Bar
of Empire Lanes, sneering as the pins go down, all at once and on cue,
with an almighty crack radiating out from Pawtucket to Geyserville;
and you knock back a codeine between gulps of fries as the
    TV overhead
shows a rerun of *Kojak* you saw a decade ago in a Canberra motel.
You are drifting, drifting ever further from Frank O'Hara's Lower East
    Side flat

where you sit daydreaming: it is 1959 and you are staring out
     the window
at a finny BelAir scarred rather nicely by kids or sleet, parked
on a billboard across the street kittycorner to a Nedick's,
the orange drink tumbling and roiling in its smudged plastic tank
a slow, piss-scented elevator ride up from the cavern
Grendel in warpaint flashes and roars through
and from which the frail sonneteer and critic of ballet
will emerge in twenty-three minutes to knock ever so delicately

just in time for a spot of Jim Beam to keep off the chill, the first
of September, as Frank puts the final touch to *Poem*
the one beginning "Khrushchev is coming on the right day!"
then kicks open the door to his study and, breathless as the
     young Rita Hayworth
after a terrible fright, cries out—*We're on with de Kooning*
for a tequila sunrise at eight, then . . . How is everyone? All right?

SHOW BUSINESS

That was a book I think you
were the Duchess
me the Stableboy
I remember now the horseapples
and itchy wool it was never that way
but God were you ever a Sireen
that I do remember and how the Townsfolk

flushed you'd have thought a gram
of niacin was in them instead of you
on your way out of the Butcher's
with half a roast and some mustard
under your arm turning suddenly
with that look of sexual malice I think
you were rich but I forget who

it was betrayed whom and were we
in love the Players most of them are
still in the Directory we could phone
and ask that is except your Sister
who perished poor thing the Actress
who took her part was gallant but missed
that delicacy of nature which killed

your Sister whom I do remember
but the rest what was between us
how the garden smelled the electric
storms were we or not I wonder
how we are punished for forgetting
or let go numb
somewhat more smooth charming and mean

BLUE AT 4 P.M.

The burnish of late afternoons
as winter ends—
this sadness coming on in waves is not round
and sweet
as the doleful cello

but jagged, intent
finding out places to get through the way wind
tries seams
and cracks of the old house, making
the furnace kick on

or the way his trumpet
sharks
through cloud and paradise shoal, nosing
out the dark fillet
to tear apart and drink his own

SUNDAY NOCTURNE

Red pulse the big jet's lights
in descent.
        The aerial
on the plumber's duplex shakes.

Along these palisades the crowded
grids subside.
           Tonight

even lawyers
and hoods
approach the foothills of reverie.

No pizza slice for the wayfarer
at this hour.
          Get thee to an inn, sport.

And still more jets,
dipping.
        From Dakar,
Akron and Samoa.
            A gentleman

in Italian loafers
disembarks.
Tomorrow at 1 he will bring
profound good news
to a steak joint in Moonachie.

I have loved the air outside Shop-Rite Liquor
on summer evenings
better than the Marin hills at dusk
lavender and gold
stretching miles to the sea.

At the junction, up from the synagogue
a weeknight, necessarily
and with my father—
a sale on German beer.

Air full of living dust:
bus exhaust, airborne grains of pizza crust
wounded crystals
appearing, disappearing
among streetlights and unsuccessful neon.

WHERE GALLUCCIO LIVED

Get all of it, boys,
every brick,
so the next big storm blows out
any ghost left with the dust.

In that closet of air the river
wind gnaws at
was where the crucifix hung;
and over there

by the radio and nails,
that's where Galluccio kept
with his busted leg
in an old, soft chair

watching TV and the cars
go past.

Whole floors,
broken up and carted off . . .

Memory stinks,
like good marinara sauce.
You never get that garlic smell
out of the walls.

ART & YOUTH

Pliny said these lights in the grass are stars;
a man walking home from his day's labor
needn't lift his head skyward to tell the signs.
Before the heavens were busy with Sputniks
and idiot beeps that say *hey!* to far-off worlds
we ran at the lights with jars. We ran and ran
until nothing was left of our bodies to spend.

An ache so sweet was born those nights
in the heat, in the grass, at summer's waning
that we try for it years later in the dance
of lust and lust's passing.
           Poor Swinburne,
dithery and gallant in great drafty rooms,
would have had this ache flogged back into him,
but the heart is soon corrupted
and love's accoutrements grow fierce.

PINNED

The ways water finds to undo
    the bonds of solid things:

you move across my flank,
    the ground turns strange;
your sylph-gang churns a breeze
    and my beanie's propeller
ticks the air morosely;
    two steps and I'm out of breath;
morsels of scrod and aspic
    drop unchewed to my plate.

Wrestlers work this way:
    they uproot you from earth
and take you back down,
    tied insolubly to their wills.

This angry bruise about to burst
on City Hall
will spend itself fast
so fluid and heat may build again.

But for a moment the light
downtown
          belongs someplace else,
not here
or any town close.

Look at the shoppers, how palpable
and bright
against gathering dark
like storied figures in stereoscope.

This is the gods' perpetual light:
      clarity
      jeopardy
         change.

SUNDAY IN NOVEMBER

And who were they all in your sleep last night
    chattering so
you'd think that when you woke
the living room would be full of friends and ghosts?

But you see, nobody's here, no one but you
    and the room's nearly bare
except for Paddy's playstring all covered in dust
and a bottle of tinted air.

Pop and Lola, the sullen little clerk from the store,
    and eight or ten more. Now
which were the dream ones and who did you meet that was
    real?
You were, for the most part, you.

Such a big room: how nice to be alone in it
    with the one lit bulb and dying plant,
the day so large and gray outside,
dogs running through it in circles, buses, shouts.

And later on where will you take her?
> *Up to the rock.* And what will you see there?
> *Roofs and the bay.* Have you a song to sing her?
> *The wind will do and she'll think it's me.*

But who were they all in your sleep last night
> first one then the next
with their menace, wild semaphore and lusts?
I hardly know where you find the strength

come morning.

At nightfall, when the inquisitive elves in elf-pants
wander over the ridge with chummy screed,
the snaps of the beak your hand becomes cease,

and evening's last fungo dwindles
high over the spruce, for an instant getting lost
in one band of sky turning dark under another,

falling back into view, falling
out of the sky, *pop*, a dead wren in his mitt. *Let's
get home*, the big boy says, *Mom'll holler.*

The car horns along Fulton subside with the dark,
the big felt-lined dark: bright little logos and cars
set in black felt while still pulsing light,

a lid on top. And see, here he comes now,
Conga Lad, pleasing the elves, who come close but not too,
making the birds go way. Time to start home,

so clean it up nice and blow germs off your pouch—
the nice warm room, the smell in the wool.

THE TREE

Pinch a branch to see if it's quick
or else the thing'll just stand
for who knows how long
sun, wind, frost, chafing it, dogs
pissing at the base
birds nesting up high where leaves had been

while the years blur
and the town next door's evacuated
so the kids don't turn stupid
from the water that solvents leached into
or testicle cancer
diagnosed in the Mayor on down

Cape Canaveral is renamed Eric Dolphy
your friends all swell, turn
ugly then drop
after their cute little girls grow up to fuck brutes
marry them and breed

but that shield of bark
photons roam the grain of
and pathogens try to corkscrew into
only to fall apart and dry . . .

because it would not bloom
because it would not die

the axman came

SUNSET IN CHINATOWN

The massive cable turns on its spool, pulling
carloads of tourists to the city's crest

       as the sun sits low
in the hills above Chinatown, exploding

suddenly in the window of Goey Loy Meats, high
along the top of the glass,

showering light over barbecued ducks—

a somehow elegiac splash
this evening, the last week before Labor Day

as if summer, in tandem with the sun,
were being pulled down

and away from us by the great spool's turning.

Thus, the sullen old man in his Mao cap
plucks the zither for change

on a crate outside the geegaw shop:

first, the ancient "Song of Cascading Water,"

followed by the plaintive
        "Lament of the Empress Ch'ou"

and even the bad little boy from Wichita Falls
trailing behind his parents in a sulk

registers that twinge

birds in the sky, insects and beasts no less
than the immortals

feel

when the plangent notes take shape in the air,
aligning their souls with Heaven and Earth.

III

LAND'S END

This air,
you say, *feels as if it hasn't touched land*
for a thousand miles,

as surf sound washes through scrub
and eucalyptus,
whether ocean or wind in the trees

or both: the park's big windmill
turning overhead
while joggers circle the ball field

only a few yards off
this path secreted in growth and mist,
the feel of a long narrow theater set

about it here on the park's western edge
just in from the highway
then the moody swells of the Pacific.

The way the chill goes out of us
and the sweat comes up
as we drive back into the heat

and how I need to take you
to all the special places, or show
you where the fog rolls down

and breaks apart in these hills or where
that gorgeous little piano bridge
comes halfway through the song,

because when what has become dormant,
meager or hardened
passes through the electric

of you, the fugitive scattered pieces
are called back to their nature—
light pouring through muslin

in a strange, bare room.

THE PARK

Jimmy the Lush,
looking rough in the shadows and dapple
of light, stares down at the ground
as his dogs take command

of the boundaries,
nuzzling turds and the air around,
snouts jerking like marionettes.
He starts off slow,

nursing a Pepsi, and keeps to his post
through the morning.
He looks almost natty, frayed Ivy League,
compared with the guys

on the corner, wasted already and screaming
about which one goes
to the Arab's next to buy more beer
and some smokes.

Then comes The Talker,
muttering softly, who finds his spot
under the loquat
and fretfully grooms in the shade.

His hat could be a military beret,
but it's far too big
and he wears it wrong, puffed
high on his head like a derby

collapsed at the edges.
They usually detonate round about two,
Jimmy first, somehow
being the senior. A pint's in him now,

high-test, and he's sore
as the dickens about something.
Once it was the mayor, once the Jews,
now it's the whole stinking planet.

The sun posts west
of the radio tower and The Talker's off
on his *possessed by space-villain X* routine,
flogging his rotors, up on his feet,

while Jimmy rails on about the ozone,
the redwoods—those bastards . . .
He spits out the *ba* sound in *bastards,*
his voice growing louder

as his breaths get short
till there's one final shriek

and then silence.

AFTER CATULLUS

(FOR THOM GUNN ON THE OCCASION
OF HIS 60TH BIRTHDAY)

Heyho, loverboy
is that a radioactive isotope you've got
burning through your shirtfront
or are you just glad to see me?

                        Chump—
you couldn't bear it at her age
much less now.
Had you supposed the years made you pliant?
Look at yourself,

flesh hanging off you
same as the old fucks you take steam with
at the gym.
Better lay off the piss, buddyboy.

Think she doesn't notice?
She sees plenty.
Ask her girlfriends. Ask the hard-bellied punks
she has it off with in the dark.

Why don't you stop licking your nuts in the corner
like an injured tom.
And quit muttering.
You knew what you were up to

when you got into this.
All of your ex-sweethearts are arranged in a chorus,
each in a pinafore with dazzling florets,
laughing themselves sick.

LATE INDIAN SUMMER

The rains hold off another week,
and the midday heat,
long after the winegrapes are in, has the cat
sprawled flat under the jade plant.

Nights already belong to winter.
You know by that tuning fork in its jacket
of bone
broadcasting to the body's far ports.

Days like this so late in the year
inflame desire, perturb
the ground of dreams, and roust us from sleep,
exhausted and stunned.

PEACHES IN NOVEMBER

Peaches redden,
and at day's end glow as if lit from within
the way bronze does,

before thudding down.
Mourning doves scatter at the sound,
shooting away in low trajectories,

and the mind starts
in spite of itself, even after weeks
of hearing them drop through the night

and all day long;
the intervals so far off any possible grid
of anticipation, and the impact

each time they hit
ground amidst a racket of leaves
just different enough

from the time before,
and the time before that, you are tricked
out of thought, awake

to the sound
as the last of them come down
and the boughs slowly raise themselves up.

SPRING TRANCES

Two snails have found the inside of a Granny Goose
Hawaiian-style potato chips,
the clipper ship on its wrapper
headed out from the islands

on a wind-swept main.
The last storms passed now, turning
to snow in the High Sierra:
they baste in their ointments deep in the tall grass,

cool among shadows and cellophane.
The sparrows and linnets have gone mad at dawn,
trilling and swooping in the branches
and ditchweed, flashing a plume

then diving; a racket
we've woken to for weeks, far too long
before the sun turns Scotch broom and the poppies to flame.
We drift through these days

half in trance from fatigue.
At evening, as the streaks of light dissolve,
we watch the boy walk home,
hatband and uniform wet from the game.

The smell of dust and sweat and the oil in his mitt
burns deep into the tissue of him.
Buffeted, drunk, wounded—
his pretty nerves bloom,

a school of minnows just under the skin.
The wind carries music up from the street,
a skewer running through him
that he slowly turns on in the scented dark.

A red band of light stretches across the west,
low over the sea, as we say goodbye to our friend,
Saturday night, in the room he always keeps unlit
and head off to take in the avenues,
actually take them in, letting the gables,

bay windows and facades impress themselves,
the clay of our brows accepting the forms.
Darkness falls over the district's slow life,
miles of pastel stucco cancelled
with its arched doorways and second-floor businesses:

herbalists and accountants, jars
of depilatories. Such a strange calm, the days
lengthening and asparagus already
under two dollars a pound.

                              Is New York fierce?

The wind, I mean. I dream of you in the shadows,
hurt, whimpering. But it's not like that, really,
is it? Lots of taxis and brittle fun.
We pass the shop of used mystery books
with its ferrety customers and proprietress

behind her desk, a swollen arachnid
surrounded by murder and the dried-out glue
of old paperback bindings.

                             What is more touching
than a used-book store on Saturday night,

dowdy clientele haunting the aisles:
the girl with bad skin, the man with a tic,
some chronic ass at the counter giving his art speech?
How utterly provincial and doomed we feel
tonight with the streetcar appearing over the rise

and at our backs the moon full in the east,
lighting the slopes of Mount Diablo
and the charred eucalyptus in the Oakland hills.
Did you see it in the East 60's
or bother to look up for it downtown?

And where would you have found it,
shimmering over Bensonhurst, over Jackson Heights?
It fairly booms down on us tonight
with the sky so clear,

                         and through us

as if these were ruins, as if we were ghosts.

WHO STOLE THE HORSES

FROM THE INDIANS?

Who stole the horses from the Indians?
my father used to ask.

     Was it you?

Oh no! I'd pipe. *Not me.*
But my father always knew.

Then there was another game:
Where are you going?

       To China, I'd announce,
Asbury Park, Hollywood.

Say hello to Dorothy Lamour. Don't forget
to write.
    And off I'd spring,
but never fast enough.
He'd catch me by the arm and haul me in.

Where are you going?
my father used to ask when I was grown.

Alaska, I would tell him,
Lisbon, Montreal.

                    You can't,
my father would tell me.
Drifters live that way.

But he was older and I was quick.
You can't, he'd say.
                    And off I'd go.

Where are you going?
my father asks,
                    and now he's old.

Vancouver, I tell him,
San Francisco, Idaho.

He just smiles sadly,
and says hardly anything at all.

A rounded and orbicular sound to it, and rings
like unto bullion—
                              the description so plagued
Mme. Cornichon's memory as she adjusted her slip
before settling herself onto the furze

for what she hoped would be reverie.
Ants scattered, two large beetles as well,
of such a kind as she had never seen,
enormous, their plates giving off an iridescent sheen

as they scuttled willy-nilly in slow-motion alarm.
Above her, hidden among leaves, the chatter
of wrens and grackles was as a fretful orison
to her in her repose, but the music that ranged

most freely through her being was Ravel's "Miroirs,"
especially so "Oiseaux tristes," suggested by the song
of a blackbird *but in the mood* of a "bird lost
in the overwhelming blackness of a forest

during the hottest hour of summer." Ah,
she remembered being awash with glissandi and arpeggios
in the salon of Princesse Edmonde de Polignac,
one afternoon with the skies outside ready to burst—

and did. But drenched as she was, shoes ruined,
she barely noticed, still so transported
by the tapestry of sound—hypnotized. Regrettably,
she took sick, and yet it was the princess,

not she, who succumbed to a bronchial complaint.
What would ever become of the great stuffed owl
suspended above the divan, the Art Nouveau sideboard
and chinoiserie? Blessedly, the illness was swift.

And the Pavane . . . What was it Ravel himself said
after a too too *adagio* performance years later?
Something about that it was the princess, not
the *Pavane*, that was supposed to be dead.

The welling of cicadas in the green
afternoon before the storm
catches on some inner ratchet along with the leaves
so dark and dense in the fading light
their color washes into surrounding air.

And when the first drops pock the dust
of the ball field next to the school,
it is not a piercing aria
or iridescent jellyfish parachuting upwards
but darkness

spreading, troweled across the diaphragm.
Every breath drags through it,
bringing in its wake a bewilderment
of fire trucks and galoshes,
the taste of pencils and Louis Bocca's ear

torn off by the fence in a game of *salugi*.

ROOMS

In the sleep that finally gives rest
I take the stairs slowly
out past the azalea dell and bison paddock,
out of view from the meadow,

and down through these rooms once more,
this endless house
under the lawns still wet from mist,
the root systems and mulch,

only to find you at a sales counter
arguing with a Russian woman.
Her English is rough but adequate,
your argument well-reasoned, controlled.

You will in the end prevail.
The salesclerk is charmed by the snatches of Russian
you mix into your conversation,
the garment exchanged for credit.

I seldom find you in these rooms anymore,
certainly not for months.
So when our eyes meet
you look momentarily bemused,

the shiver of surprise softening to pleasure.
You are lovely,
somewhat older than I remember,
business-like in a tailored suit.

Our conversation is courtly,
flirtatious in what we imagine an Old World way.
How strange to encounter you here
in this harsh light, the tableau

of a downtown department store with its cases
of perfumes, gels and leather goods.
And how inexplicably refreshed I feel afterward
lying here alone,

awakened precisely as our commerce ended
by the shouts of children going to school.

WATCHING DOGWOOD BLOSSOMS FALL

IN A PARKING LOT OFF ROUTE 46

Dogwood blossoms drift down at evening
        as semis pound past Phoenix Seafood

and the Savarin plant, west to the Turnpike,
        Paterson or hills beyond.

The adulterated, pearly light and bleak perfume
        of benzene and exhaust

make this solitary tree and the last of its bloom
        as stirring somehow after another day

at the hospital with Mother and the ashen old ladies
        lost to TV reruns flickering overhead

as that shower of peach blossoms Tu Fu watched
        fall on the riverbank

from the shadows of the Jade Pavilion,
　　　　while ghosts and the music

of yellow orioles found out the seam of him
　　　　and slowly cut along it.

The skylight silvers
and a faint shudder from the underground
travels up the building's steel.

Dawn breaks across this wilderness
of roofs with their old wooden storage tanks
and caps of louvered cowlings

moving in the wind. Your back,
raised hip and thigh
well-tooled as a rounded baluster

on a lathe of shadow and light.

SUNDAY, ACROSS THE TASMAN

Big weather is moving over the headlands.
Turrets and steeples jab up at it
and the bank towers stand rooted,
logos ablaze at the edge of the earth.

In a suburban church basement the AA faithful
are singing hymns of renewal, devotion
and praise. He struggles with his umbrella
in the lobby of the Art Deco theater,

a dead ringer for the old 72nd Street Loew's
with its plaster Buddhas and kitsch arabesques—
the Preservation Society's last, best stand.
Young couples walk past hand in hand

as golden oldies flood onto the sidewalk
from the sweatshirt emporium next door.
His heart bobs, a small craft
awash for a moment with nostalgia.

Bartok liked to pick out a folk melody
and set it, a jewel in the thick
of hammered discords and shifting registers:
not unlike this dippy Mamas and Papas tune

floating along nicely among the debris.
The rain turns heavy, and the first
of the night's wild southerlies keens through,
laying waste the camellia and toi toi.

He wonders how the islanders managed
in their outriggers: if they flipped
or rode it through, plunging
from trough to trough with their ballast

of hoki, maomao, cod. Time for a drink.
A feral little businessman shakes
the bartender's left breast in greeting,
amiably, old friends.

                Hi, Jack—she says.

Country people, he thinks, mistakenly.
The routines of home seem a lifetime away
and the scenes of his life rather quaint:
an old genre flick, never quite distinct

enough or strange to be revived
except on TV, and then only very late,

with discount-mattress and hair-transplant ads.

Strange to be among them in the noon sun
with their fabulous night histories,
the welter and crush of downtown tableaux
above Second Avenue or at the Hotel Earle,
honeycomb of lambent episode.

Big silence in the midday heat
except for insect whir and a passing car:
you imagine them under the sandy ground,
under the slate and granite markers,
and pretend to hear, faintly at first,

as if through the woods at night,
the stream of delicious talk,
the rages, dishing and whispered come-ons,
the posturing and retort
at that murderous cocktail party, the '50s,

Speed and Nerve presiding
right before it blew into a camp B-movie
cavalcade of car wrecks, lithium

and broken hearts

                    (soundtrack by Schoenberg
and Elmer Bernstein). The afterglow of them:
neon on a sunny day—

                       celluloid in flames,
the fried image and random splice,
wild parabolas, butchery.

IV

Green first thing each day sees waves—
the chair, armoire, overhead fixtures, you name it,
waves—which, you might say, things really are,
but Green just lies there awhile breathing
long slow breaths, in and out, through his mouth
like he was maybe seasick, until in an hour or so
the waves simmer down and then the trails and colors
off of things, that all quiets down as well and Green
starts to think of washing up, breakfast even
with everything still moving around, colors, trails
and sounds, from the street and plumbing next door,
vibrating—of course you might say that's what
sound really is, after all, vibrations—but Green,
he's not thinking physics at this stage, nuh-uh,
our boy's only trying to get himself out of bed,
get a grip, but sometimes, and this is the kicker,
another party, shall we say, is in the room
with Green, and Green knows this other party
and they do *not* get along, which understates it
quite a bit, quite a bit, and Green knows
that this other cat is an hallucination, right,
but these two have a routine that goes way back

and Green starts hollering, throwing stuff
until he's all shook up, whole day gone to hell,
bummer . . .

        Anyhow, the docs are having a look,
see if they can't dream up a cocktail,
but seems our boy ate quite a pile of acid one time,
clinical, wow, enough juice for half a block—
go go go, little Greenie—blew the wiring out
from behind his headlights and now, no matter what,
can't find the knob to turn off the show.

SNOW IN NORTH JERSEY

Snow is falling along the Boulevard
and its little cemeteries hugged by transmission shops
and on the stone bear in the park
and the WWI monument, making a crust
on the soldier with his chin strap and bayonet
It's blowing in from the west
over the low hills and meadowlands
swirling past the giant cracking stills
that flare all night along the Turnpike
It is with a terrible deliberateness
that Mr. Ruiz reaches into his back pocket
and counts out $18 and change for his LOTTO picks
while in the upstairs of a thousand duplexes
with the TV on, cancers tick   tick   tick
and the snow continues to fall and blanket
these crowded rows of frame and brick
with their heartbreaking porches and castellations
and the red '68 Impala on blocks
and Joe he's drinking again and Myra's boy Tommy
in the old days it would have been a disgrace
and Father Keenan's not been having a good winter
and it was nice enough this morning

till noon anyhow with the sun sitting up there like a crown
over a great big dome of mackerel sky
But it's coming down now, all right
falling on the Dixon-Crucible Pencil factory
and on the spur to Bayonne
along the length of the Pulaski Skyway
and on St. Bridget's and the Alibi Saloon
closed now, 'ho dear, I can't remember how long
and lordjesussaveus they're still making babies
and what did you expect from this life
and they're calling for snow tonight and through tomorrow
an inch an hour over 9 Ridge Road and the old courthouse
and along the sluggish, gray Passaic
as it empties itself into Newark Bay
and on Grandpa's store that sells curries now
and St. Peter's almost made it to the semis this year
It's snowing on the canal and railyards, the bus barns and trucks
and on all the swells in their big houses along the river bluff
It's snowing on us all
and on a three-story *fix-up* off of Van Vorst Park
a young lawyer couple from Manhattan bought
where for no special reason in back of a closet
a thick, dusty volume from the '30s sits open
with a broken spine and smelling of mildew
to a chapter titled *Social Realism*

THE DOG STOLTZ

The dog Stoltz pushed his paw pads into my neck,
the warm, beaten leather deep under my chin,
and let slip the one paw to up near my mouth
with all the filth of the many blocks we trod,
together trod, a well-moistened, adenoidal sound,
part sigh and part growl, coming out of him,
transported, he seemed, in a slow-motion delirium
as I tickled his chest and behind his ear
when he just then told me he'd tear out my throat,
looked in my eye and smiled, best as a dog can,
then turned ruminative and spoke once more:
—*I simply have to knock off that essay on Sassoon.*
This would have been Sassoon the war poet, understand.
Dogs cannot write. My mother told me this.
As for his talk, well, I took no special notice.
His love of the war poets was well known.
Stoltz would have been part bull and something else.
Two friends walked by just then, handily as these things go,
and inquired of us sitting down there on the stoop,
not even, a doorway merely, along a busy street,
how went the day and what pursuits was I attending;
but what interested the two of them most

were the tergiversations of the dog Stoltz,

first beast, then scholar, then abject and adored.

(Say, who among us does not care to be undressed?)

He was not really my dog, you see, and of this made note,

but were glad as well at my having a new dog in my life.

It was a busy stretch of pavement, Amsterdam maybe,

or Broadway, or farther down just south of Chelsea.

I can tell you it was the West Side, of that I'm certain,

and it was mild, spring-like, a few drops in the air.

The friends passed along and the dog Stoltz slept.

He was not my dog, you know. He simply followed me out

of what can only have been a very fine home,

such were his graces, his recondite tastes.

But he was a killer too, and rather smelled.

I cannot accommodate another animal now, please understand.

I am between places. I will yearn for Stoltz, but no.

SILVER GELATIN

He was watching, looking down at the park
from the 14th floor, waiting.
There is an hour, an afternoon light
well along into winter.

The angle she made with the pram
as she moved past the fountain
could not possibly be improved upon.
Her black hat,

the fur collar and padded shoulders—
a solitary young domestic,
caught through a net of griseous branches,
is getting the baby home for dinner,

home long before dark.
It is terribly cold.
She leans forward, pushing in haste.
At her own now extreme angle

and with the black coat and hat,
the pram underneath her,
the snow underfoot,
she looks, for all the world, from here,

a broken-off piece of Chinese ideogram
moving across the page.

UTTAR PRADESH

You were dozing over Uttar Pradesh
well after the shadows of Annapurna
swept across the big plane's starboard wing,

dreaming a peevish little dream
of Stinky Phil, your playground tormentor
from fifty years before, his red earmuffs

and curious cigar voice vivid as the tapioca
you used to gag on at the end of Thursday lunch,
when the captain's serene, patriarchal voice

suggested you buckle up, moments before
the plane jumped then yawed in an air pocket
and dropped five hundred feet. Oh shit,

there goes the Parcheesi board and what's left
of a very bold Shiraz. Melissa
purses her lips in the compact mirror,

turns a quarter left, then right a tad,
scowls at her mascara and snaps it shut with a sigh.
You are the preeminent colorist

of your era. Some would suggest a fraud
with your grand chevelure of white hair and cape.
Mother would certainly not disagree,

but here you are again, crossing continents,
six miles above the petty quarrels,
the tossed green salads and car wrecks

to receive yet another prize, a ribbon,
a princely sum in a foreign capital
and a spread on the Sunday culture page.

How very far away now seem your student days:
happy, hungry, cooking up manifestos,
turpentine, pussy, stale cigarette smoke.

It was evident from the start. It screamed
at you from billboards, fabric shops, museums;
and no one else saw it, no one but you.

Amazing. Then half a lifetime to execute it
in paint. What a long time with one idea.
But still, it was a doozy, put you

in the art books and kept you there for life.
There will be a car waiting when you arrive.
Kremer is visiting with the Philharmonic

and will do the Sibelius, your favorite.
You recall meeting him some years ago
at a dinner in—Cologne, I think it was.

An intense young man, but very pleasant.
Right, now you remember the evening,
the lugubrious molding and burgundy drapes . . .

Ah, yes, and a most memorable *hasenpfeffer*.

The planet may have tilted, if only a hint
when the shelf of cloud burnt angrily
before dusk
         jack-o'-lantern stuff

her hair the color of her coat,
fall wear

        ■

The wet stain her bathing suit left
on the bench
         the shape of Bolivia,
drying, drying into atolls
Ursa Minor, a thumbprint

        ■

It was at Herbie's place, no
Pinckney's, she showed us her pubes
and long shadow of thigh

The fresh linen smelled so sunnily like
What did the lady on TV call it?

An orchard of some kind

■

Sure it's just like staring
out the window, Johnny
sure

but with fly eyes
and sidewise

■

When Pappy and Mahoney left
for dinner and a show

I was soooo a-LONE
there in the doorway, sore way
of being the phone ringing

It was summer again and green

■

You do turkey, baby, I like peas
snap beans, oyster sauce, fuzzy

blond roux

■

The clues to my being—
the bloody windsprint

the mashie niblick hanging
from a willow

the retreating aria

■

The way the *spaldeen* jumped left
instead of right

and died on your square of sidewalk
that Friday afternoon so long ago

That's all you need to know

■

Oh, I was freed
freed, I say

kneeling, teething

chopchopchopping
like a tractor piston

like an outboard coughing up lake

ON FIRST LOOKING INTO

JOSEPH CORNELL'S DIARIES

The sopressata fée outside of Calfasso's
with the swept-back 'do and blood on her smock
grabs a quick smoke on the sidewalk,
tosses it in the gutter then sucks back her lips
till they smack, getting her lipstick right.
                              Fierce little thing . . .
My freight elevator makes a distant whump
then squeals to a stop on one of the floors back there
behind my left ventricle.
                    OUT OF SERVICE
for months, I am at first alarmed then refreshed.

                    ∎

What a preposterously spring-like day on Anderson Avenue
for the depths of February.
                    You can hear the snow melt
under the parked cars, and the #4 School crossing guard,
burly and mustachioed, reminds me just then
of an elderly Victor McLaglen, a favorite of the children
and somewhat stooped in his waning years
but ever that loyal and gallant pal from *Gunga Din*.

■

Try as I might now for weeks I still cannot find
the space I need to contain the Clorox label
which would go behind and to the right
of the orange box of gelatin stool softeners.

■

There is that and the far larger dilemma,
one that has resisted me and my wiles for years:
to find a distillate or tincture
of daytime TV commercials for the ladies—
Pond's cold cream, say, or diaper rash powders—
then somehow reconstitute and *fashion the flavor*
to a doctor's waiting room and a blue plastic chair
(in the modern Italian design style)
with a splayed, greasy *Mademoiselle*
from the previous June left underneath.

(Oh, but if I could only unknot that one
every arroyo and vista would open up to me)

I go park awhile outside the boarded-up Dairy Queen
and try to find Fauré's *Berceuse.*
                                        A gust of wind
rocks the car, just perceptibly,
and then it comes to me, is served up to me, really:
warm butterscotch syrup and the Little League parade.

■

My *condition* intrudes
and all the air goes right out of me.
It is the bad feeling. I call it *Dolph*.
It smells of roofing tar and makes my pineal gland itch,
itch till it aches.

It spreads into my extremities and lays waste my strength
so that never again will my inventions come to life:

that little green chutney bottle in a field of stars
and the doll's taffeta apron . . .

nor will I bathe ever again with the divine Mavlakapova
in my special Thursday dream.

GRAY LIGHT IN MAY

The soft gray light between rains
This enveloping light
Under a canopy of green
Oak   chestnut   maple
Last night the moon, orange and full
Over Manhattan's West Side
Edgewater below so sleepy
The neighborhood asleep
My family asleep
Coming back here how many years now
And the ride in from Newark
Manhattan looming over the meadows
The beauties of travel are due to
The strange hours we keep to see them
This soft windless air
Away now nearly thirty years
You can smell the tidal flats below
Passenger jets silent overhead
In and out of Kennedy, LaGuardia
As if gliding across the night
My heart abrim
A glass of wine, spilling over

The air like wine
I am a stranger to myself

The soft gray light
The still moist air
The azaleas in these yards
Under the canopies of leaves
Fiercely abloom in this gray light
Between rains
Almost stereoscopic
The broad green leaves overhead as well
Painters know it, photographers too
The smell of lilac
Nudging my chest like the muzzle of a dog
The manner in which this gray light
Wraps itself around things
Saturating them
Bringing up their color
So much a part of me
So much of what is dearest
I can barely stand upright under the weight of it
The song of the wood thrush
Reverberates through the heavy air
And around its hidden columns
Who knows the Palisades as I do
Lilac and dogwood

Flowering pear blossoms, mingling
Drifting in gutters
How many years
For how many years
A stranger to my own heart

WEST

An apocalyptic crack spreads like thunder
over sintered gorges and alkali flats.
The junco is knocked sideways then drops
as if shot onto a granite bed, turning
slowly mahogany there—wild peony.
Somewhere in the bleached sky and cirrus a Phantom
is at play, singeing cattle, lifting shingles
off farmhouse roofs. An enormous ball
of phosphorus bounds across the Carson Sink.

—Christ, it was hot out there on Jackass Flats
after that big wave of wire, sagebrush
and rattlesnakes broke over us.

The Paiute flint auger fairly hummed
with chromium when they pulled it out of Stillwater Marsh.
You could listen to it like a conch shell,
an impossibly busy, serial music
that compounds and accelerates, on and on.

THEY OFTTIMES CHOOSE

I

They ofttimes choose to pause naked at the door
if in the morning they are well pleased,
then turn with a flourish back to their toilette.

I have more than the one time beheld,
whether Corinna, Meg or Philomel,
that grand, nay, regal posture till my gaze

was snared in hers and tenderly led down,
that I might see, might know one moment more
the abundance there flesh can barely contain—

oh, the freshets, the unaccountable dolors—
then she, with one long last ferocious look,
would burn me deep yet leave no wound or pain.

Then take their leave but are not truly gone,
for amidst the cushions and disarray
bracelets and earrings, a kerchief I'll find.

They, who are not careless in other ways,
are careless neither in what they leave behind
as well as where. For when I spy it there

half-hidden in a fold or by an emptied glass
they are already several hours passed
from my mind as well as last embrace

but return now in full if not in flesh.
How well these ladies do contrive, how well,
to keep me in thrall with their sweet neglect.

MONSTERS

. . . and thus of what she earst had beene
Remayned nothing in the worlde.

OVID, *Metamorphoses*
Translated by Arthur Golding

Lie down then with the monsters
Take your ease
They frightened you once
But not anymore
You awaken among them
A changeling of sorts
Attended first by Infant Esau
Then the Sirenoforms
Who jabber and squeal
Through breached sternums
Waving their dorsal flaps
Noisily sucking
I saw you spoon out the giblets
To Zoophagous Margie
Heard you coo ever so sweetly
Like an indulgent mommy

At her guttural chuckling
Then wipe clean the spittle
From her mouth and chin
I watched you there
Thriving
As if among your own
An hysteria gaining
With drink and time
So flushed with pleasure
At the fact of your presence
Your comeliness and bearing
How they primped
And what a fuss they made
Over your choker
Your jacket
Your hair
How you inflamed them
Till appetite crackled
Fat in the skillet
Clementine the Pigboy
Could not help but touch you
Your hips and arms
Your breasts
I turned away
And you said nothing
Emboldened, then Zep, Jo-Jo

And the Crocodile Girl too
Still you said nothing
And the noise
You had to have seen me
But for the din
Might have heard me
Call to you
Call out your name

SOMEONE NAMED GUTIERREZ:

A DREAM, A WESTERN

Outside the cantina
with you in the backseat of a ruined DeSoto,
torn upholstery, vinyl mange
and the big old radio's static frying
what could only be a Dixie Cups tune.
Things had gone terribly bad,
and Slim, who drove us the whole long way
through chaparral and dust,
was in there now, with them,
asking for the money he had no right to,
had no right to even ten years back
when the fire was, or so he says.
They nearly killed him then,
the fool, the braggart, the Suicide Kid,
just itching after a good old-timey
late afternoon cowboy send-off,
blood and gold and glinting sidearms,

with us stuck back there yet, hove-to
in the backseat like two kids
waiting for Dad.
                          When you touched me,
the lightest of touches, the most unforeseen,
carelessly along the wrist.
I nearly came unglued.
I mean, I knew about Ramon,
that lovely boy—and for so long,
the two of you. I cherish that photo still,
your white tam-o'-shanter, his red TransAm.
Then I became water.
Then, from what had once been my chest,
a plant made of light effloresced.
Thus, our adventure began, our slow-motion
free fall through the vapors and oils.
I stammered at your white flesh.
                                And that,
that's when the shooting began.

TOYS

The janitor washing the blackboard
in Mrs. Turnaud's class

February night not too far
from the border with Vermont

snowless, and still a little stoned

thinks he caught a patch
of aurora borealis out the window

or maybe just a headlight off a cloud

■

Thank you for kissing me just then
It was getting to be rather a swarm in there
with the tendrils, suckers and shoots

no purpose, no end in sight

syntax a lost dynasty

■

That child is in terror
terror of himself

You can tell by his face
how it's wrong in three parts

and with a helmet of busy bruised air
framing it

the parents, insensible
walk chattering behind

He's going to hurt himself
He's going to hurt himself, soon

■

Look at the colored liquids and string beans
in a jar, pickled

the carved mahogany sideboard

so old and so dark, like Europe

■

The gaunt timpanist
with the visiting symphony orchestra

sits by himself on a concrete bench
in the abandoned pedestrian mall

Sunday with dead oak and maple
leaves skittering past

in this lovely provincial city
renowned for its love

of the arts

■

She's a drunkard but still pretty
40-ish, oddly athletic

The sidewalk might as well be
the top of a sawhorse
she walks so daintily with her pint
in a small brown bag

when suddenly a terrific boom
ripples across the sky overhead
brilliant afternoon

It's the celebrated Blue Angels
rocketing east to west
in their Tomcat fighters

nearly on top of each other
tight diamond formation

their contrails feathering behind
come apart and vanish into sky

■

The hobbyist in his room, alone
under the blue turret

his work of many years now done

each row of matchsticks flawlessly
joined, canted, plumb

the fading smell of epoxy

THE CONVERSATION

This then was the conversation
There were others, of course, not a few
But there was this one
Time and again
The one that truly mattered
And the others, well
I can barely remember the others
But this one
That drove all ahead of it
A great wave or wind
That tore apart the very ground
That sent up a wall of debris
That would leave nothing
Could leave only nothing
By design
If asked
If one could ask a brute thing
Inquire of rock or bone
Entreat
Put one's own arm
One's hand
Down into the engine of its force

To know its workings
Even if torn to pieces
To have felt down there
Felt something
Move
An intelligence of parts
Gear and ratchet
Anything
But not this
No, not this, ever, no
Only the fact of it
This whirlwind
Why not
A biblical reek to it
Perfect
But scaled down
Way down
And kept in the vestibule
An ornament
A kinetic sculpture
In the corner
On a stand
An *objet d'art*

BEFORE DAWN ON BLUFF ROAD

The crow's raw hectoring cry
scoops clean an oval divot
of sky, its fading echo
among the oaks and poplars swallowed
first by a jet banking west
then the Erie-Lackawanna
sounding its horn as it comes through the tunnel
through the cliffs to the river
and around the bend of King's Cove Bluff,
full of timber, Ford chassis, rock salt.

You can hear it in the dark
from beyond what was once the amusement park.
And the wind carries along as well,
from down by the river,
when the tide's just so,
the drainage just so,
the chemical ghost of old factories,
the rotted piers and warehouses:
lye, pigfat, copra from Lever Bros.,
formaldehyde from the coffee plant,

dyes, unimaginable solvents—
a soup of polymers, oxides,
tailings fifty years old
seeping through the mud, the aroma
almost comforting by now, like food,
wafting into my childhood room
with its fevers and dreams.
My old parents asleep,
only a few yards across the hall,
door open—lest I cry?
                    I remember
almost nothing of my life.

DIABLO: A RECIPE

[FOR W. S. DI PIERO]

Caro mio, the hot must dwell among the dark
the orange habanero

burning like a candle in a terra-cotta jar
and the onion tuned, just so

that when the mud commences to bubble, to streak
and to spit, a barely audible sweetness

is there too; but still, still
that torrid little fist commands

the temperate hand, the wooden spoon, the meats
nothing will avail

but patience, as in many things
in love, say, or with a poem

but in this the most of all
for as the first of afternoon's late shadows falls

and as I-95's muffled rumbling
ebbs and flows in the distance, crossing the river

beyond the big beech tree, its leaves flaring gold
only now, after how many hours

the meat and marrow slip from the bone
the dark pasilla and chorizo show

as currents in a muddy river show
only a shade or two off

but careful not to turn the lights on
or all of it is lost

for the broth and the room are now as one
one fabric of shadow

broken only by the blue flame of the burner
turned very low

and so, the moment has come
for the first, the most important glass of wine

a big red, why not a Merlot
because only now, alone in this room

dark and quiet as a chapel
the garlic has slowly begun to bloom

and the wine in the back of your throat
will be made sonorous by it

then it is time, after much stirring
and some contemplation

to find the appropriate tune
perhaps one of Schubert's final sonatas

and take up your spoon once more
and for the first time taste

how the ferocious one, the brute
because of the lily has been seduced

and burns still, indelibly
but like the small blue flame in the darkened room

Red pear leaves take the light at four,
and a patch of brick on the south, rear wall
stripped of wisteria: the two reds embering
a little while then dying back into the shadows.
A corner of the afternoon is all,
maybe half an hour, not much more—
October, November . . . the beech tree bare now.

Sunday's blow would have done it.
And always the Interstate out there, like surf,
running up to Boston or south to New York.
And broken-up city across the river,
a used-to-be textile port, gutted.
One good high-rise, an old-style stepback,
and the power plant on Point Street,

glowing orange now in sodium light,
highlines feeding out of it, dripping
with porcelain isolators. We watch it every night,
red lights blinking from the three tall stacks,
the staggered sequence of its flashing crowns
scaring off the geese and Cessnas.
The turbines and generators roar, never ceasing.

We went inside. We saw it. We heard.
He made us lean underneath and see the flame
through the thick glass, deep in the steel.
And then we went back into the wind,
past the Nightingale Metals truck
and across the bridge on foot. No one saw.
No one knows. The eyes of the beech.

We have examined these afternoons
like a slide taken from a petri dish,
spindles of living matter, degraded, fraying,
taking on new shapes, gray, opalescent.
The red lights in the distance, blinking.
The roar in the boiler house.
The drawn shades.

SELF-PORTRAIT

It was a *lost* dream, a bridges and heights
and headed home dream, but too long,
far too long and mazy and all the wrong tone.
And then there was that station, so massive,
with its tiers, platforms, girders and steps,
trains rushing through on the express track,
filled to bursting, commuters illuminated,
each face vivid, highlighted—is that you?—
exasperation, fatigue, concern at the time.
But the time was all wrong; it was late,
way late, the station ready to close.
The subways never close, you say, even in dreams:
empty, only rarely if ever a train, but open.
This was no ordinary station, or dream.

You could see Manhattan in the far distance,
big towers beyond the raggedy miles
of tenements, viaducts, frozen playgrounds.
Like the view from the Nor'easter headed south
as it winds its way around the Bronx,
right before it dips down into the tunnel.
But this place would have had to be in Queens.

At the start it was a plane I was headed for,
headed for that morning from quite another town.
This must be the old *train to the plane,*
the one that lets you off way out by Kennedy.
But that got shut down years ago.
Now I was far from anything, Jersey especially.
I always head back to Jersey in a pinch.

My two suitcases were gone as well, both black,
one large, one small. My shoes too, also black.
There I was, lost, weaving left and right,
pitiful as a bug caught out in the light.
Way down there in the bowels with the gated-up
shoe-shine, burger and newsstands, a cop, a drunk.
But a barbershop of sorts still open and lit
and oddly partitioned into three distinct rooms:
one with a man fitting rubber skin skulls
onto mannequin heads; the next a barber
fussily attending to three bald heads;
the next what could only be a tiny morgue,
but with those very same heads from the barber's,
only this time like death masks of Renaissance popes.

That's when I ran onto this burly black guy,
security or some kind of station chief.
He was short with me for being there but nice enough

and led me on a search for my two bags.
Through horrible rooms: bodies, gunnysacks,
leavings from some old and gruesome jumble sale.
—*The two last rooms on earth,* I heard myself say.
And still no bags, but when I looked down
there were my shoes, back on my feet again,
except each from a different pair. Odd, that,
but I was plenty glad to have them on,
stuck by myself in the middle of nowhere
with the station shutting down for the night
and who knows what waiting out there in the shadows.

Somehow it had gotten to be dawn.
I found myself standing up to my ankles in weeds
with rusted fenders and a torn-down fence.
Manhattan sticking up in the filmy distance.
Lots of birds, planes too, out of Kennedy.
When two ugly-looking kids were headed my way.
Didn't like how this was shaping up at all.
If I had to bolt, the weeds would hold me back.
But they turned out to be sweet, bewildered boys,
in wonderment at my simply standing there.
I believe I had on a flannel shirt, a plaid,
sun igniting the wet, dark smells of earth.
It was all so eerily gentle and strange
I might as well have been Captain Cook in the Marquesas.

V

The markets never rest
Always they are somewhere in agitation
Pork bellies, titanium, winter wheat
Electromagnetic ether peppered with photons
Treasure spewing from Unisys A-15 J mainframes
Across the firmament
Soundlessly among the thunderheads and passenger jets
As they make their nightlong journeys
Across the oceans and steppes

Nebulae, incandescent frog spawn of information
Trembling in the claw of Scorpio
Not an instant, then shooting away
Like an enormous cloud of starlings

Garbage scows move slowly down the estuary
The lights of the airport pulse in morning darkness
Food trucks, propane, tortured hearts
The reticent epistemologist parks
Gets out, checks the curb, reparks
Thunder of jets
Peristalsis of great capitals

How pretty in her tartan scarf
Her ruminative frown
Ambiguity and Reason
Locked in a slow, ferocious tango
Of *if not, why not*

THE OLD POET, DYING

He looks eerily young,
what's left of him,
purged, somehow, back into boyhood.
It is difficult not to watch
the movie on TV at the foot of his bed,
40˝ color screen,
a jailhouse dolly psychodrama:
truncheons and dirty shower scenes.
I recognize one of the actresses,
now a famous lesbian,
clearly an early B-movie role.
The black nurse says "Oh dear"
during the beatings.
—*TV in this town is crap*, he says.
His voice is very faint.
He leans toward me,
sliding further and further,
until the nurse has to straighten him out,
scolding him gently.
He reaches out for my hand.
The sudden intimacy rattles me.
He is telling a story.

Two, actually,

and at some point they blend together.

There are rivers and trains,

Oxford and a town near Hamburg.

Also, the night train to Milan

and a lovely Italian breakfast.

The river in Oxford—

he can't remember the name;

but the birds and fritillaria in bloom . . .

He remembers the purple flowers

and a plate of gingerbread cookies

set out at one of the colleges.

He gasps to remember those cookies.

How surprised he must have been

by the largesse,

and hungry, too.

—He's drifting in and out:

I can hear the nurse

on the phone from the other room.

He has been remembering Europe for me.

Exhausted, he lies quiet for a time.

—There's nothing better than a good pee,

he says and begins to fade.

He seems very close to death.

Perhaps in a moment, perhaps a week.

Then awakes.

Every patch of story, no matter how fuddled,
resolves into a drollery.
He will perish, I imagine,
en route to a drollery.

Although his poems,
little kinetic snapshots of trees and light,
so denuded of personality
and delicately made
that irony of any sort
would stand out
like a pile of steaming cow flop
on a parquet floor.
We are in a great metropolis
that rises heroically from the American prairie:
a baronial home,
the finest of neighborhoods,
its broad streets nearly empty
on a Saturday afternoon,
here and there a redbud in bloom.
Even in health,
a man so modest and soft-spoken
as to be invisible
among others, in a room of almost any size.
It was, I think, a kind of hardship.
—*Have you met what's-his-name yet?*

he asks.

        You know who I mean,
the big shot.

           —*Yes,* I tell him, *I have.*
—*You know that poem of his?*
Everyone knows that poem
where he's sitting indoors by the fire
and it's snowing outside
and he suddenly feels a snowflake
on his wrist?
He pauses and begins to nod off.
I remember now the name of the river
he was after, the Cherwell,
with its naked dons, The Parson's Pleasure.
There's a fiercesome catfight
on the TV, with blondie catching hell
from the chicana.
He comes round again and turns to me,
leaning close,

        —*Well, of course,* he says,
taking my hand,
his eyes narrowing with malice and delight:
—*That's not going to be just any old snowflake,*
now, is it?

THE SWIMMER

[FOR BRIGHDE]

The japonica and laurels tremble
as the wind picks up
out the west-facing wall of the old natatorium,
made wholly of glass.
The swimmer takes her laps,
steady and sure through a blur of turquoise
and importunings of chlorine.
The large room itself now darkens,
lit as it is by natural light,
as the storm clouds press closer toward land.

Back and forth, the solitary swimmer,
now on her second mile,
is caught up, held almost,
in that one element she finds her ease;
and in moving through it
the very edges of her strength are engaged,
until, on a turn, her breathing stretched,
health pours into her.

The great glass wall, first pilloried by drops,
their dull, pellet-like clack,
is now streaming with rain:
and from this hill,
where, half-hidden, the old rec center sits,
across the sixty rolling blocks to the sea,
all that is material and solid,
the houses, the cars, the trees,
diminish into shadow
and continue to recede till there is nothing,
nothing at all in the world,
but water.

A BEAUTIFUL MIND

We pushed a tiny catheter and shunt
right through what looked to be a "propitious bump"
on the skull and into the left hemisphere
of the frontal lobe, way back there,
right above the Sylvian fissure, in the speech area.
And went in again, a long reacher,
all the way back in the temporal lobe,
further along that same stretch of crease,
just behind the ear
and snug up under the collateral sulcus.
Then jerry-rigged a causeway of sorts between them.

You can imagine the mess
and attendant motor disturbance—
flashing lights, dogs barking, sirens.
Like I knew what I was doing, right?
Well, call it two parts dowsing, five parts backhoe.
It was Murph lent me his putty knife;
that is, after I dropped my own.
Ran into a patch of static electricity down there
just about made my hair stand on end.

What I had in mind—*arrrgh, arrrgh*—
was something along the lines of stereophonic sound,
except with words, and more like *wraparound*.
What you might call synergy-enhancement surgery,
one language center communing with another:
Dr. Broca, meet Dr. Wernicke, like so,
but in new, multiple and unforeseen ways.

Sure, the two had their voltage-gated ion channels,
their desultory whispered chitchats,
Post-it notes along the connective fibers.
But you've seen the flow diagrams: paltry, niggling stuff.
I've had it with all that,
the parsimonious back and forth between X and Y,
like an insufferably long, indirect taxi ride
between Waterloo Station and West Finchley.
I'm talking time, tedium, the bludgeoning expense.

So I drop down in there with my Davey lamp,
lay down some cable, have a good look-see.
Mercy, Miss Percy, it's worse than the back of your TV.
Might as well have left the trepan set at home.
Never seen anything like it, I tell you what.
Press down there, the eyes start tearing;
down back in there, the willie jumps up and you turn beet red.
Messing about, you can imagine what happens next:

Your blistering corolla's ventriloquisms

Sepulveda, der phu-duh-duh

                              Knell, wet stencil

          Ocarina thirst

All of that digging only to arrive in Hell:
an endless tape-loop of the aphasic's broken rant,
Friday night forever in the Indeterminists' Revival Tent.

The beauty—
the way the swallows gather around the Duomo
for a few moments at dusk then scatter,
darting away across the Vale
with its checkerboard pastels dissolving into smoke
along with the hills beyond.
We saw it that one time from the Maestro's apartments,
through a little oval window above the piazza
while that awful American baritone—what's his name—
was mauling the love duet with Poppea at the end,
and she so wickedly angelic, a Veronese angel . . .
When de Kooning, drunk, crashed into us,
then the lot of us staggering off to that bar
overlooking the Ponte delle Torri
and finally drinking in the dawn outside Vincenzo's.
I remember the violist and cor anglais
enjoying some passion in the doorway.
Didn't they later marry? Perhaps not.
And the mezzo from Winston-Salem—
I won't tell you her name; you'll know it.

She was only a girl then, pretending
to be native, with her Neapolitan accent
and dark looks, that extravagant manner
and big laugh the divas all seem to cultivate.
But then she was only a girl, peeking
to check if her act was really coming off.
These actresses and stage performers are always a trial.
By the time you get them home
and properly unwound, the cockerels and tweety birds
already at it, they either collapse
into tears or fall dead away, shoes still on,
snoring and farting like drunken sailors.
But that night, that night it was the English poet
(now much beloved but in those days known as the *Badger*)
who was after her, her and her friend,
the pianist from Ravenna, the quieter one,
the heart-attack brunette, renowned for her Saint-Saëns.
You'll know her name too, and the recordings
she made later on with the mezzo of the Schubert lieder.
But then they were just kids, figuring it out,
suffering dainty little sips
of that tall awful yellow drink, a favorite here,
meanwhile taking the measure of it all,
as if rehearsing for a more important moment down the road.
The cunning, energy and fortitude of these creatures
almost never fails to horrify and amaze,

especially two thoroughbreds like these.
One might easily hate them for it,
but as well hate some magnificent cat in the tall grass
scanning the savanna for signs of meat.
Anyhow, the *Badger* was on form that night.
You wouldn't know him. He was young then,
really quite presentable, even appealing, I suppose,
with a shock of blond hair
and that pale distracted feral look he chose to wear.
I don't know that I've ever seen a human being drink like that.
I mean now the swollen old cunt could pass for Uncle Bertie
but in those days . . . Anyhow, the *Badger*
was well along into his routine: a few bons mots,
feigned interest, the learned quote and the rest,
then his signature:

   —I don't suppose a fuck would be out of the question?
The girls took no notice, giggling between themselves
and the inevitable band of toffs and toff-y rent boys
who gather round these things. Love culture,
the toffs, can't live without it: mother's milk,
penicillin for the syphilitic.
And where would we all be without them: their dinners,
soirees, art openings, their expensive drink;
and whose appalling wives could we so generously appall?
Can't get enough of it, these toffs. Or the wives.
So this particular evening the *Badger* was right on chart,

watching, waiting, picking his spot:

        —Ha, ha, listen, I don't suppose . . .

when just then Signore Cor Anglais struggles to his feet,

humongous hard-on like a prow in advance of the rest,

and proceeds to blow a heavenly riff from Bruckner,

one of those alphorn bits the Bavarians so adore.

Well now, this provoked an enormous display

on the part of the toffs, sissies, remittance men,

expats—those orphans, those sorry deracinated ghosts—

the lot of them in the ruins of black tie,

shrieking like 8-year-olds at the circus

when the clown takes a flop, out of their gourds,

full up with helium, *Eeeeeeeeee—*

la vie bohème, right out there on the Corso,

a moment to be savored and regurgitated for years to come,

when the cor anglais decides to pass out,

Signora Viola all over him, beside herself,

like the final scene from—well, you name it—

the toffs, etc., carrying on like they had a ringside seat

at Krakatoa erupting on New Year's Eve;

and then I hear the mezzo—all of us,

everything else falling away, the air rippling with it—

up on her feet, singing the "Adagiati, Poppea,"

that lullaby of foreboding the nurse Arnalta delivers

in Monteverdi's *L'incoronazione*, warning

of the iniquitous union ahead, but sung

with such tenderness, an unearthly sweetness.
The entire street falling silent around us,
and the *Badger* just sitting there like the rest,
hypnotized, but now his face gone slack:
astonishment? epiphany? grief? but clearly shaken
and—unimaginably out of character—about to weep.

Imagine in all the debris of space
The countless trade names
    Jugurtha   *Tuolumne*   *Chert-Farms*
Some of these belong to you
Can you tell which ones
Each has its own sequence of microtones
Together they make up a kind of tune
Your tune
The ceiling and walls are star maps
Breathing, alive
Those aren't stars, darling
That's your nervous system
Nanna didn't take you to planetariums like this
Go on, touch
Lovely, isn't it
Like phosphorus on Thule Lake
Sweet summer midnights
Shimmery, like applause under the skin
Can you make it out
Almost a hiss
An old shellac LP of white noise

Playing in the distance
Foolish, troublesome boy
That hapless adventuring of yours
Be very still
Now can you hear it

You ask, Aristippus, and I tell you
it's in the waiting; that the moment, like a stag,
may arrive at your doorstep as if from a cloud
and disappear before you know it,
not even the after-trace of a phantasm;
and you will have missed it for all of your scheming,
your daydreaming about lofty verses and fame,
your lunging and casting about like a spaniel
barking his way into the middle of a slough,
then unable to get out.

                       For all of your many laurels,
you wouldn't recognize it if it bit you on the ass.
You'd mistake it for some starstruck slattern
crudely making a pass. It's really hopeless, you know.
You haven't the temperament, never did.
Where you belong is in the rag trade,
wholesale, plenty of volume. There's the action,
steady too, and regular hours:
push, and push hard enough, you've got it made.

Not like this wretched, unforgiving game,
where you can sit around for months sniffing

at the air like a patient in a convalescent ward
for mentals: knackered, reamed, a source
of amusement for all the neighbors to see.
It really is humiliating, I'm telling you.
In the end, what it comes down to is appetite—
the enforced idleness, the solitude:
nothing, hectares of nothing, litanies of nothing on microfiche.

It's simply not your line.
You're standard issue, old boy, but with claws.
If not the wholesale trade, maybe politics or law.
Trust me, Calliope, Erato—they're both twisted sisters.
Six months of Hildegard von Bingen, migraines, et al.,
next day it's Captain Cunt of the Roaring Forties,
grinding and tossing like to break your back in two.
Give it up, you old windbag. Be on your way.
The weather here stinks, and neither of these girls is for you.

CHRISTMASTIME IN CORONADO

The attack jets come in low
over the ocean
past the tennis courts and the Duchess's cottage,
in tandem
low over the Navy golf course
headed for the North Island airstrip
then wheel to the left
out over the water again,
the afternoon's last light
making a movie set of the offshore islands
around and back once more
past the grand old wooden hotel and its cupolas
with a series of watery, high-pitched *whups*
as they cut back their engines
and disappear over the ridge.

The town seems very still, almost empty, rich.
Christmas displays in store windows.
A goodly stream of cars.
The traffic lights make a sound too, bird-like.
I often get confused.

The roaring overhead. The traffic noise.
There is no place to go.

Out on the Silver Strand
the joggers and sweethearts take in the sunset
the air overhead as busy as war
Skyhawks, Vigilantes, Intruders
the cargo and surveillance planes
sub hunters, gunships
Phantom, Tomcat, Cobra . . .
It must have given the late President
great succor out there in his compound
those long troubled evenings in San Clemente
to see the lights
and track the arc of the distant thunder
as he sat, with a drink, looking
out that enormous window at the sea, the stars
a blur of light from the distant pier.

I have read, of the late President
from those who had been close to him, through it all
that he had in him a reflective
one might even say philosophical cast of mind.
I wouldn't know to say it wasn't true.
I wouldn't know to say.
But I myself have been thinking constantly of America.

Only of late, only here
with the might of the nation roaring overhead
around the clock
spewing vapor from their strakes
going fucking nowhere
and noisily coming back.

[1998]

April of that year in the one country
was unusually clear
and with *brisk* northeasterlies
"straight from the Urals."
Their ancient regent at long last succumbed
and laid to rest after much ceremony.
Sinatra was everywhere that spring,
in the hotel lobbies, toilets, shops—
"Fly Me to the Moon," "You Make Me Feel
So Young," name it.
On TV a computer-generated Weimaraner
sang "I Did It My Way"
in a gravelly barroom baritone.
         —He only weighed 130 lbs.,
Ava Gardner was to have remarked,
soaking wet,
but a hundred of those lbs. was cock.

Whereas, the season before
in the other country to the west
no matter into which room you walked
it would have been the *heart-wrenching adagietto*

from Mahler's *Symphony No. 5*.
Only a small country,
it had endured a long, *famously tragic* history.
Still, it was more than passing strange,
not halfway through your plate of mussels,
the tremblingly _____ adagietto,
showering you with the debris
of Gustav Mahler's *tortured* soul. True,
wife Alma was a troublesome slut;
we know this of her and choose to forgive.
But what of this late Romantic excess,
this anthem of the Hapsburg twilight,
in a cruelly served and windswept land?

We had only lately come over the Sally Gap
across the bogland, down through the glen,
and were walking slowly
along the Lower Lake of Glendalough.
Afternoon had turned toward evening,
and with it came a chill.
And with the chill a mist
had begun to gather over the lake.
—*This is a haunted place*, I heard her say.

It was quiet then. We were the last ones there.
Only a patch of birdsong. Only the wind.

Unheeded, from somewhere *out of the blue,*
—*Liberace*, she said, and nothing more.
We continued on our walk and listened,
if just to the silence.
This would have been an hour St. Kevin knew
and savored
before retreating to the Gatehouse
and into the monastery for evening prayer.
One can imagine a stillness forming around him there
like those halos of gold or ocher
that surround the sacred figures in frescoes.

Much as they do with "Lee"
in one of his brocaded lamé jumpsuits
with its sequins catching the spotlights,
enorbing the performer in brilliant rays
as he smiles *coquettishly* to the Vegas crowd
then turns to deliver the first
in a series of *thunderous* glissandi,
somehow finding his way back
to a climactic, *magnificently rousing* chorus
of that million seller
and *timeless classic,*

"Moon River."

THE SINGLE GENTLEMAN'S CHOW MEIN

The ants are very bad tonight
and the poison is old.
It's the rains that bring them out,
you know. The first big storm
and there they are,
all over the counter and with their scouts
in advance, under the sink mat
and mason jars, probing
the way they do.

They have a smell, of that I'm certain,
a formic aroma,
that gathers round them in the heat
of their frenzy; I don't know
but that they take it on outside
and bring it along with them
on their journey through these walls.

But they do enjoy it, the bait.
It must still have some strength.
See how they cluster.
You need only stir the paste

with the end of a match
and the arsenic's perfume blooms again.
They really do love it.
Watch how they feed.
Soon they will take the poison back
from where they have come,
back to their nest,
and destroy their queen.

I only ordered half a pound this time.
Most evenings—yes, most—
I would probably get a whole and leave some
for lunch next day,
perhaps a casserole.
But just tonight it was looking,
well, a trifle sad,
sitting there in its steam tray
for half an eternity.

You know how it tends to get slow
after the lunch trade.
The one batch in its grease for hours,
taking on that viscous, cloudy look,
almost jaundiced under the fluorescent lights.
From time to time the homeless wander in
and bargain for some rice,
perhaps a spear of wilted broccoli.
And if it's quiet, the Lotus will oblige.

But I do like it.
I add things on, you see:
vegetables, all manner of condiments
and treats, a shrimp
or scallop, or two, or three.
It's very nice the way I do it,
and never the same way twice.

They know me down there,
at the Lotus, I mean,
and have done for years.
The girls behind the counter change.
—*Ah, ha, chow mein,*
they say, smiling, when they know me.
It's quite nice, really.
One of them, oh, three years back
was a stunner, terribly pretty;
taking a night course, as I recall.
—*You look like professor, no?*
she said to me one day, a trifle severe
in delivery but very sweet.
I've never been with a Chinese.

The large black man is dancing
He is dancing in his head
On the stage of the Salle Pleyel
And the Parisians are watching
As he takes one step to the left
But, look, his foot is not touching
The ground, as if it's too hot
Or cold, or not to be found there at all
Then slamming it down
And spinning round
Like a drunk in his funny hat

The large black man is dancing
On the stage of the Salle Pleyel
He has gotten up from the piano
And begun his silly dance
Lurching, first one way, then . . .
Wait, he is changing his mind
Frozen there in space, on just one leg
His drummer and bass, Pierre,

That is, and Claude, puzzling through
What he has left behind
Soldiering on, regardless
Wondering where they misplaced the time
On the stage of the Salle Pleyel

The large black man is dancing
Dancing in his head
On the stage of the Salle Pleyel
And hundreds of French are watching him
Twitch or swat
Away an imaginary chord in order to make room
For the next, with a pirouette
Courtly as a maitre d' on roller skates

The large black man, the large
Black man is dancing
And the Parisians are watching
Nervously. But the drummer, Pierre
That is, and Claude on bass
Are beginning to get it
They are watching the black man's dance
And think they've found it
Relax, *mes chers*
We are nearing the end of the tune

The black, black man is dancing
Dancing in his head
On the stage of the grand *théâtre*
And the lovers of jazz are there
They are out there in force
Watching the black man from America
Watching the black man dance
It is 1954
And the tune is "Trinkle, Tinkle"
What are they to do
What to make
Of the black man up there dancing
Is he *fou*
Does he not know where he is or who
Is in the audience watching
There is the editor of *Jazz Hot*
Section C, Aisle 12, Seat #2
He will be confused, no
Is he being made the fool
What are they all to do

Pierre and Claude, the drummer,
That is, and the contrabass
They think: O.K., I've got it
Where the accents drop
Where not

And those very weird spaces between
(*Ha, ha, ha,* but not really)

The large black man
In his coat and his tie
And the funny little hat
And crazy grin
The large black man is
Dancing

It's simply untrue, Maecenas, that I do not care for nature.
A vile canard: I do, but not unadorned. I need architecture, streets,
and, not least, the human form, to frame, contrast and ornament.
A birch among a sea of birches does not enchant.
Rather, give me a birch, say, over there in the moonlight,
to the left of the belvedere, by itself or part of a small stand,
with ample space around to show off its charms to advantage.
Hey, now, spare me the *decadent* and *jaded* bit, old dear.
You like your little Claudia's tits and ass all the better
when they're showcased and partially hid by those ribbons of silk.

You see that storm headed our way from the southwest,
those dark clouds blowing in at an angle like an advance guard,
racing across the sky above the Medical Center?
One needs those featureless blocks up there, I tell you,
to provide us with the theater, the spectacle of it.
A front coming in over any old hill is no big deal,
only another patch of rotten weather.
But check out the values there, in the charcoal-bellied, mottled clouds
and how they blend or stand against the pale stone of the towers,
or how that stone fares in the storm's particular light.
There's more art in that than your insipid vineyards,
being driven half mad by blackflies, dodging rattlers.

Just watch how the eucalyptus twist and writhe in the wind,
tossing their crowns and branches like the dancers we saw—when was it?—
the other night. Nature takes its metaphors from city life,
and the other way round, each diminished when left to its own devices.
But of the two, it's town, I say, proves better for poetic figures,
not least because nature is to be found in any city you look,
if only a pitiful avocado plant on a shelf somewhere,
dragging its rhizomes in a highball glass. Nature is always there,
indoors and out: a cat, a pigeon, a phthisic sweet gum,
not to mention the sky. A city has its very own weather,
altogether different from the nearby countryside.
And a moon is never so pretty as in a poisoned sky.
Besides, every city has a park, its own public greensward
with flowers and trees. How much of that does one really need?

There's good reason why the folks you find up-country tend to be dull.
It's because they spend their days talking to animals, you know.
Listen, don't get me wrong, I think all those songbirds are great:
the waxwing's trill and rattle, the warbler's hoarse little *chuif.*
Perfectly delicate, marvelous stuff, an overture to cocktails.
But the birdsong for me, right up there with Bartók and Monk,
is never straight up but part of a mix—footsteps, traffic,
fountains, shouts—that beggar Cage or Stockhausen.
Accident, contingency: it's *city* nature, Maecenas, that's for me,
not those endless manured fields, lowing cattle and whatever sheep do.
I'd like to once walk through those hills you go on about
without getting shit all over my shoes. You leave that part out.

Frankly, I'm nauseated by these bucolic rhapsodies
you and your kind indulge yourselves with and the public eats up.
Exactly who do you think you're fooling? You're city boys,
one and all, and with your apartments still in town, as well,
so you can slip back in for a secret shag and proper meal after.
You're in town, Maecenas, more than you will comfortably admit.
C'mon, babe, it's me, Augie-boy, friends since we were kids.
But hey, I'm not unamused at the rustic posture you affect,
the mud-splattered wellingtons, the coarse fabric of your pants.
Your conversation, the pleasures of your table, remain a delight,
at least so long as I can make it back to town that same night.
But please, I'm begging, Maecenas, show an old friend some respect:
spare me the update on feed prices, these lectures on the good life.

ON WAKING IN A ROOM AND NOT

KNOWING WHERE ONE IS

There is a bureau and there is a wall
and no one is beside you.
Beyond the curtains only silence,
broken now and again by a car or truck.
And if you are very still
an occasional drip from the faucet.
Such are the room's acoustics
it is difficult to place exactly where from.
Also, the tick of the clock.
It is very dark.
There exist all manner of blacks,
lampblack, for instance,
much favored by the ancients,
so deep and so dense
and free of any shades of gray
or brown. But this,
this dark is of another order,
compounded of innumerable shadows,
a weave of them.
One is able to make out shapes.

It is not restful, to be like this, here,
nor is it a fearful place.
In a moment or two you will know
exactly where you are,
on which side the door,
your wallet, your shoes,
and what today you'll have to do.

Cities each have a kind of light,
a color even,
or set of undertones
determined by the river or hills
as well as by the stone
of their countless buildings.
I cannot yet recall what city this is I'm in.
It must be close to dawn.

CHRISTMAS IN CHINATOWN

They're off doing what they do
and it is pleasant to be here without them
taking up so much room.
They are safely among their own,
in front of their piles of meat, arguing
about cars and their generals,
and, of course, with the TV going all the while.

One reads that the digestive wind passed by cattle
is many times more destructive to the atmosphere
than all of the aerosol cans combined.
How does one measure such a thing?
The world has been coming to an end
for 5,000 years. If not tomorrow,
surely, one day very soon.

R_X FOR S

Nap. Go looking for the fox
in Holland Park at dusk. And if you see him,
and he sees you, well then.
Smoke even more ganj, and at hours
you're unaccustomed. Nothing
must be allowed to interfere
with this, your willed indolence.
Set forth among your dreams as a traveler
in a distant rain forest, awonder
at the hibiscus-like carnivorous blooms
spangling the tendrils and moss.
They nor the sleek ebony *jrdaka*
will bite, nor even give affront
because you are swaddled in a cloud,
a molecular raiment of scent
by which they will know you.
The world is full, full of care,
grief but another tortured littoral,
hostage to the sea and rough weather.
Decamp to the sheltered valleys.
You will find comfort there, and safety,
and, for no reason, remember a colored plate

belonging to a favored storybook
your father would read to you
when you were only a very small girl.
Sleep.

THE BUS BARN AT NIGHT

Motion is not a condition
but a desire
to be outside of one's Self
and all desire must be swept away

so saith fatso Gautama
bus-like
under the shade of some shrub
in the Deer Park
in some grove
some municipal greensward
chewing a leaf
that has left him stoned
as a stone
stone-like
mouthing this sententious drivel
some errand boy
some rich man's son
dutifully sets down
on a dusty tablet
ignoring the insects and snakes

After midnight
under the arc lights

like a giant soundstage
the abandoned set
of an action spectaular
Mrs. Kiniski's team
goes bus to bus
hoovering candy wrappers
crumbs
and then with their scrapers
attending to the grease
and impacted filth
and gum
as Rudolfo sluices away
in the southeast corner
and the boss, with a sigh
comes to the end
of Hermann Hesse's *Siddhartha*

Phalanx upon phalanx
of impassive Buddha-wagons
silver hulls and red trim
Fleet of the Three Jewels
the Attainment & Perfection
City Transit Corp.
hosed down, lubricated and tuned
in the Eternity Shop
the Cave of Illumination and Fumes

At the gates to the Hereafter,
a rather drab affair, might as well be a union hall
in south Milwaukee, but with shackled
sweating bodies along the walls,
female, chiefly, and not at all miserable,
straining like bored sultanas at their fetters,
each of them singing a separate song.
A Semitic chap—the greeter, I suppose—
gives me the quick once-over
and most amused he seems to be. Has me figured.
Not unlike a gent I met only last week,
a salesman at a stereo shop on Broadway.
—*So*, he says. Nothing more.
—*Sew buttons*, says I, in a cavalier mood
and why not.

        Ushers me into a tiny cinema,
a two-seater, really quite deluxe,
a great big Diet Coke in the cupholder,
fizzing away.

        —*O.K.?* he asks.
I nod and the film unrolls.
A 20-million-dollar home movie it is,

featuring yours truly: at the foot
of the stairs with the dog, mounting
Josette in a New Smyrna love nest,
a fraught kitchen showdown with Mom,
the suicide, car wreck, home run.
You know what these things are like:
the outlandish hairdos, pastel bathroom fixtures.
The editing is out of this world,
the whole shebang in under an hour:
the air-raid drill on Wednesday morning,
1957, when Tito wet his pants;
there I am, beside myself with laughter,
miserable little creature.
The elemental, slow-motion machinery
of character's forcing house.
Even with all the fancy camera angles,
jump cuts and the rest,
might as well be a chain of short features:
Animal Husbandry, Sexual Hygiene,
Lisboa by Night . . .
What a lot of erections, voidings, pretzels,
bouncing the ball against the stoop.
She really did love you, all along.
These jealousies and rages of yours,
like a disgusting skin condition
that never entirely goes away.

You, you . . .
What catalogs of failure, self-deception . . .
And then the lights come back on,
likewise the choir's splintered polyphony,
with its shards of *Sprechstimme*, the Ronettes, whatnot,
and in the air around us
something like the odor of a freshly spent cartridge,
when my minder asks brightly,

> *—How about another Coke?*

I would rather have been Dufy
with these sails and darkening clouds—
well, not Dufy, and this is not *Le Sud*:
better, say, Cranach,
had he been given to painting sails
against the day's last light.
Perhaps there is a kind of sail in Mary's eyes,
poor thing.
          The Baltic night is moving in,
dragging its somber quilt behind
like a filthy bridal train.
I would rather have enacted this in paint,
have the brushstrokes tell
what just passed through,
brightly at first
and then not, a glove of shadow across my sternum.

How much there is to know, to find,
should one step into the water and dive deep down
with a lamp and Baedeker,
a floor plan of the spirit museum
with its black onyx cloisters and galleries

that open one on the next
filled with jawbones, beetles, fiery gems,
tapestries almost water, immaterial,
bleeding signs.

       Then set it down in paint,
the blacks, the greens and browns;
not explain.
Cumbersome words: imprecise, always hurrying
to catch up and never quite.
But further, further still:
even the painter must be destroyed
in order that one may become the paint.

THE TARTAR SWEPT

The Tartar swept across the plain

In their furs and silk panties

Snub-nosed monkey men with cinders for eyes

Attached to their ponies like centaurs

Forcing the snowy passes of the Carpathians

Streaming from defiles like columns of ants

Arraying their host in a vasty wheel

White, gray, black and chestnut steeds

10,000 each to a quadrant

Turning, turning at the Jenuye's command

This terrible pinwheel

Gathering speed like a Bulgar dance

Faster and faster

Until it explodes, columns of horsemen

Peeling away in all the four directions

Hard across the *puszta*

Dust from their hooves darkening the sky

They fall upon village and town

Like raptors, like tigers, like wolves on the fold

Mauling the *zsa-zsas*

And leaving them senseless in puddles of goaty drool

Smashing balalaikas

Ripping the ears off hussars and pissing in the wounds

They for whom the back of a horse

Is their only country

For whom a roof and four walls is like unto a grave

And a city, *ptuh*, a city

A pullulating sore that exists to be scourged

Stinky dumb nomads with blood still caked

On shield and cuirass

And the yellow loess from the dunes of the Takla Makan

And the Corridor of Kansu

Between their toes and caught in their scalps

Like storm clouds in the distance

Fast approaching

With news of the steppes, the lagoons and Bitter Lakes

Edicts, torchings, infestation

The smoke of chronicles

Finding their way by the upper reaches

Of the Selinga and the Irtysh

To Issyk-Kul, the Aral, and then the Caspian

Vanquishing the Bashkirs and Alans

By their speed outstripping rumor

Tireless mounts, short-legged and strong

From whose backs arrows are expertly dispatched

As fast as they can be pulled from the quiver

Samarkand, Bukhara, Harat, Nishapur

More violent in every destruction

This race of men which had never before been seen

With their roving fierceness

Scarcely known to ancient documents

From beyond the edge of Scythia

From beyond the frozen ocean

Pouring out of the Caucasus

Surpassing every extreme of ferocity

From the Don to the Dniester

The Black Sea to the Pripet Marshes

Laying waste the Ostrogoth villages

Taking with them every last cookie

Then dicking the help

These wanton boys of nature

Who shot forward like a bolt from on high

Routing with great slaughter

All that they could come to grips with

In their wild career

Their beautiful shifting formations

Thousands advancing at the wave of a scarf

Then doubling back or making a turn

With their diabolical sallies and feints

Remorseless and in poor humor

So they arrived at the gates of Christendom